Dickens Charles

Oliver Twist

Tome 1

Richard Bentley

1839

Y2 27423

NEW WORK BY "BOZ."

BARNABY RUDGE:

BY "BOZ."

Which will be published forthwith in BENTLEY'S MISCELLANY.

OLIVER TWIST.

BY

CHARLES DICKENS.

AUTHOR OF "THE PICKWICK PAPERS."

SECOND EDITION.

IN THREE VOLUMES.

VOL. I.

LONDON.

RICHARD BENTLEY, NEW BURLINGTON STREET.

1839.

LONDON:
PRINTED BY SAMUEL BENTLEY,
Dorset Street, Fleet Street.

OLIVER TWIST.

CHAPTER I.

TREATS OF THE PLACE WHERE OLIVER TWIST WAS BORN, AND OF THE CIRCUMSTANCES ATTENDING HIS BIRTH.

AMONG other public buildings in a certain town which for many reasons it will be prudent to refrain from mentioning, and to which I will assign no fictitious name, it boasts of one which is common to most towns, great or small, to wit, a workhouse; and in this workhouse was born, on a day and date which I need not take upon myself to repeat, inasmuch as it can be of no possible consequence to the reader, in this stage of the business at all events, the item of mortality whose name is prefixed to the head of this chapter. For a long time after he was ushered into this world of sorrow and trouble, by the parish surgeon, it remained a matter of considerable doubt whether the child would survive to bear any name at all; in which case it is somewhat more than probable that these memoirs would never have appeared, or, if they had, being comprised within a couple of pages, that they would have possessed the inestimable merit of being the most concise and faithful specimen of biography extant in the literature of any age or country. Although I am not disposed to maintain that the being born in a workhouse is in itself the most fortunate and enviable circumstance that can possibly befal a human being, I do mean to say that in this particular instance it was the best thing for Oliver Twist that could by possibility have occurred. The fact is, that there was considerable difficulty in inducing Oliver to take upon himself the office of respiration,— a troublesome practice, but one which custom has rendered necessary to our easy existence,— and for some time he lay gasping on a little flock mattress, rather unequally poised between this world and the next, the balance being decidedly in favour of the latter. Now, if during this brief period, Oliver had been surrounded by careful grandmothers, anxious aunts, experienced nurses, and doctors of profound wisdom, he would most inevitably and indubitably have been killed in no time. There being nobody by, however, but a pauper old woman, who was rendered rather misty by an unwonted allowance of beer, and a parish surgeon who did such matters by contract, Oliver and nature fought out the point between them. The result was, that, after a few struggles, Oliver breathed, sneezed, and proceeded to advertise to the inmates of the workhouse the fact of a new burden having been imposed upon the parish, by setting up as loud a cry as could reasonably have been expected from a male infant who had not been possessed of that very useful appendage, a voice, for a much longer space of time than three minutes and a quarter.

As Oliver gave this first proof of the

free and proper action of his lungs, the patchwork coverlet which was carelessly flung over the iron bedstead, rustled; the pale face of a young female was raised feebly from the pillow; and a faint voice imperfectly articulated the words, " Let me see the child, and die."

The surgeon had been sitting with his face turned towards the fire, giving the palms of his hands a warm and a rub alternately; but as the young woman spoke, he rose, and advancing to the bed's head, said, with more kindness than might have been expected of him—

" Oh, you must not talk about dying yet."

" Lor bless her dear heart, no !" interposed the nurse, hastily depositing in her pocket a green glass bottle, the contents of which she had been tasting in a corner with evident satisfaction. " Lor bless her dear heart, when she has lived as long as I have, sir, and had thirteen children of her own, and all on 'em dead except two, and them in the wurkus with me, she'll know better than to take on in that way, bless her dear heart! Think what it is to be a mother, there's a dear young lamb, do."

Apparently this consolatory perspective of a mother's prospects failed in producing its due effect. The patient shook her head, and stretched out her hand towards the child.

The surgeon deposited it in her arms. She imprinted her cold white lips passionately on its forehead, passed her hands over her face, gazed wildly round, shuddered, fell back—and died. They chafed her breast, hands, and temples; but the blood had frozen for ever. They talked of hope and comfort. They had been strangers too long.

"It's all over, Mrs. Thingummy," said the surgeon at last.

"Ah, poor dear, so it is!" said the nurse, picking up the cork of the green bottle which had fallen out on the pillow as she stooped to take up the child. "Poor dear!"

"You needn't mind sending up to me, if the child cries, nurse," said the surgeon, putting on his gloves with great deliberation. "It's very likely it *will* be troublesome. Give it a little gruel if it is." He put on his hat, and, pausing by the bed-side on his way to the door, added

"She was a good-looking girl, too; where did she come from?"

"She was brought here last night," replied the old woman, "by the overseer's order. She was found lying in the street;—she had walked some distance, for her shoes were worn to pieces; but where she came from, or where she was going to, nobody knows.".

The surgeon leant over the body, and raised the left hand. "The old story," he said, shaking his head: "no wedding-ring, I see. Ah! good night!"

The medical gentleman walked away to dinner; and the nurse, having once more applied herself to the green bottle, sat down on a low chair before the fire, and proceeded to dress the infant.

And what an excellent example of the power of dress young Oliver Twist was! Wrapped in the blanket which had hitherto formed his only covering, he might have been the child of a nobleman or a beggar;—it would have been hard for the haughtiest stranger to have fixed his station in society. But now that he was enveloped in the old calico robes, which had grown yellow in the same service, he was badged and ticketed, and fell into his place at once—a parish child—the orphan of a workhouse—the humble half-starved drudge—to be cuffed and buffeted through the world, despised by all, and pitied by none.

Oliver cried lustily. If he could have known that he was an orphan, left to the tender mercies of churchwardens and overseers, perhaps he would have cried the louder.

CHAPTER II.

TREATS OF OLIVER TWIST'S GROWTH, EDUCATION, AND BOARD.

For the next eight or ten months, Oliver was the victim of a systematic course of treachery and deception—he was brought up by hand. The hungry and destitute situation of the infant orphan was duly reported by the workhouse authorities to the parish authorities. The parish authorities inquired with dignity of the workhouse authorities, whether there was no female then domiciled in " the house" who was in a situation to impart to Oliver Twist the consolation and nourishment of which he stood in need. The workhouse authorities replied with humility that there was not. Upon this, the parish authorities magnanimously and humanely resolved, that Oliver should be " farm-ed," or, in other words, that he should be despatched to a branch-workhouse some three miles off, where twenty or thirty other juvenile offenders against the poor-laws rolled about the floor all day, without the inconvenience of too much food or too much clothing, under the parental superintendence of an elderly female who received the culprits at and for the consideration of sevenpence-halfpenny per small head per week. Sevenpence-halfpenny's worth per week is a good round diet for a child; a great deal may be got for sevenpence-halfpenny—quit enough to overload its stomach, and make it uncomfortable. The elderly female was a woman of wisdom and experience; she knew what was good for children, and she had a very accurate perception of what was good for herself. So, she appropriated the greater part of the weekly stipend to her own use, and consigned the rising parochial generation to even a shorter allowance than was originally provided for them; thereby finding in the lowest depth a deeper still, and proving herself a very great experimental philosopher.

Everybody knows the story of another experimental philosopher, who had a great theory about a horse being able to live without eating, and who demonstrated it so well, that he got his own horse down to a straw a day, and would most unquestionably have rendered him a very spirited and rampacious animal upon nothing at all, if he had not died, just four-and-twenty hours before he was to have had his first comfortable bait of air. Unfortunately for the experimental philosophy of the female to whose protecting care Oliver Twist was delivered over, a similar result usually attended the operation of *her* system; for at the very moment when a child had contrived to exist upon the smallest possible portion of the weakest possible food, it did perversely happen in eight and a half cases out of ten, either that it sickened from want and cold, or fell into the fire from neglect, or got smothered by accident; in any one of which cases, the miserable little being was usually summoned into another world, and there gathered to the fathers which it had never known in this.

Occasionally, when there was some more than usually interesting inquest upon a parish child who had been overlooked in turning up a bedstead, or inadvertently scalded to death when there happened to be a washing, though the latter accident was very scarce,—anything approaching to a washing being of rare occurrence in the farm,—the jury would take it into their heads to ask troublesome questions, or the parishioners would rebelliously affix their signatures to a remonstrance: but these impertinences were speedily checked by the evidence of the surgeon, and the testimony of the beadle; the former of whom had always opened the body and found nothing inside (which was very probable indeed), and the latter of whom invariably swore whatever the parish wanted, which was very self-devotional. Besides, the board made periodical pilgrimages to the farm, and always sent the beadle the day before, to say they were going. The children were neat and clean to behold, when *they* went; and what more would the people have?

It cannot be expected that this system of farming would produce any very extraordinary or luxuriant crop. Oliver Twist's ninth birth-day found him a pale thin child, somewhat diminutive in stature, and decidedly small in circumference. But nature or inheritance had implanted a good sturdy spirit in Oliver's breast: it had had plenty of room to expand, thanks to the spare diet of the establishment; and perhaps to this circumstance may be attributed his having any ninth birth-day at all. Be this as it may, however, it *was* his ninth birth-day; and he was keeping it in the coal-cellar with a select party of two other young gentlemen, who, after participating with him in a sound threshing, had been locked up therein for atrociously presuming to be hungry, when Mrs. Mann, the good lady of the house, was unexpectedly startled by the apparition of Mr. Bumble the beadle striving to undo the wicket of the garden-gate.

"Goodness gracious! is that you, Mr. Bumble, sir?" said Mrs. Mann, thrusting her head out of the window in well-affected ecstasies of joy. " (Susan, take Oliver and them two brats up stairs, and wash 'em directly.)—My heart alive! Mr. Bumble, how glad I am to see you, sure-ly!"

Now Mr. Bumble was a fat man, and a choleric one; so, instead of responding to this open-hearted salutation in a kindred spirit, he gave the little wicket a tremendous shake, and then bestowed upon it a kick which could have emanated from no leg but a beadle's.

" Lor, only think," said Mrs. Mann, running out,—for the three boys had been removed by this time,—" only think of that! That I should have forgotten that the gate was bolted on the inside, on account of them dear children! Walk in, sir; walk in, pray, Mr. Bumble, do sir."

Although this invitation was accompanied with a curtsey that might have softened the heart of a churchwarden, it by no means mollified the beadle.

" Do you think this respectful or proper conduct, Mrs. Mann," inquired Mr. Bumble, grasping his cane,—" to keep the parish officers a-waiting at your garden-gate, when they come here upon pòrochial business connected with the porochial orphans? Are you aware, Mrs. Mann, that you are, as I may say, a porochial delegate, and a stipendiary?"

"I'm sure, Mr. Bumble, that I was only a-telling one or two of the dear children as is so fond of you, that it was you a-coming," replied Mrs. Mann with great humility.

Mr. Bumble had a great idea of his oratorical powers and his importance. He had displayed the one, and vindicated the other. He relaxed.

"Well, well, Mrs. Mann," he replied in a calmer tone; "it may be as you say; it may may be. Lead the way in, Mrs. Mann, for I come on business, and have got something to say."

Mrs. Mann ushered the beadle into a small parlour with a brick floor: placed a seat for him, and officiously deposited his cocked hat and cane on the table before him. Mr. Bumble wiped from his forehead the perspiration which his walk had engendered, glanced complacently at the cocked hat, and smiled. Yes, he smiled: beadles are but men, and Mr. Bumble smiled.

"Now don't you be offended at what I'm a-going to say," observed Mrs. Mann, with captivating sweetness. "You've had a long walk, you know, or I wouldn't mention it. Now will you take a little drop of something, Mr. Bumble?"

"Not a drop — not a drop," said Mr. Bumble, waving his right hand in a dignified, but still placid manner.

"I think you will," said Mrs. Mann, who had noticed the tone of the refusal, and the gesture that had accompanied it. "Just a *leetle* drop, with a little cold water, and a lump of sugar."

Mr. Bumble coughed.

"Now, just a little drop," said Mrs. Mann persuasively.

"What is it?" inquired the beadle.

"Why, it's what I'm obliged to keep a little of in the house, to put in the blessed infants' Daffy when they ain't well, Mr. Bumble," replied Mrs. Mann as she opened a corner cupboard, and took down a bottle and glass. " It's gin."

" Do you give the children Daffy, Mrs. Mann?" inquired Bumble, following with his eyes the interesting process of mixing.

" Ah, bless 'em, that I do, dear as it is," replied the nurse. " I couldn't see 'em suffer before my very eyes, you know, sir."

" No," said Mr. Bumble approvingly; " no, you could not. You are a humane woman, Mrs. Mann."—(Here she set down the glass.) —" I shall take an early opportunity of mentioning it to the board, Mrs. Mann."—(He drew it towards him.)—" You feel as a mother, Mrs. Mann."—He stirred the gin and water.)—" I—I drink your health with cheerfulness, Mrs. Mann;"—and he swallowed half of it.

" And now about business," said the beadle, taking out a leathern pocket-book. " The child that was half-baptized Oliver Twist, is nine year old to-day."

"Bless him!" interposed Mrs. Mann, inflaming her left eye with the corner of her apron.

"And notwithstanding a offered reward of ten pound, which was afterwards increased to twenty pound,—notwithstanding the most superlative, and, I may say, supernat'ral exertions on the part of this parish," said Bumble, "we have never been able to discover who is his father, or what is his mother's settlement, name, or condition."

Mrs. Mann raised her hands in astonishment; but added, after a moment's reflection, "How comes he to have any name at all, then?"

The beadle drew himself up with great pride, and said, "I inwented it."

"You, Mr. Bumble!"

"I, Mrs. Mann. We name our foundlins in alphabetical order. The last was a S,—Swubble, I named him. This was a T,—Twist, I named *him*. The next one as comes will be Unwin, and the next Vilkins. I have got names ready made to the end of the alphabet, and all the way through it again, when we come to Z."

"Why, you're quite a literary character, sir!" said Mrs. Mann.

"Well, well," said the beadle, evidently gratified with the compliment; "perhaps I may be—perhaps I may be, Mrs. Mann." He finished the gin and water, and added, "Oliver being now too old to remain here, the Board have determined to have him back into the house, and I have come out myself to take him there,—so let me see him at once."

"I'll fetch him directly," said Mrs. Mann, leaving the room for that purpose. And Oliver, having by this time had as much of the outer coat of dirt, which encrusted his face and hands, removed, as could be scrubbed off in one washing, was led into the room by his benevolent protectress.

"Make a bow to the gentleman, Oliver," said Mrs. Mann.

Oliver made a bow, which was divided between the beadle on the chair and the cocked-hat on the table.

"Will you go along with me, Oliver?" said Mr. Bumble in a majestic voice.

Oliver was about to say that he would go along with anybody with great readiness, when, glancing upwards, he caught sight of Mrs. Mann, who had got behind the beadle's chair, and was shaking her fist at him with a furious countenance. He took the hint at once, for the fist had been too often impressed upon his body not to be deeply impressed upon his recollection.

"Will *she* go with me?" inquired poor Oliver.

"No, she can't," replied Mr. Bumble; "but she'll come and see you sometimes."

This was no very great consolation to the child; but, young as he was, he had sense enough to make a feint of feeling great regret at going away. It was no very difficult matter for the boy to call the tears into his eyes. Hunger and recent ill-usage are great assistants if you want to cry; and Oliver cried very naturally indeed. Mrs. Mann gave him a thousand embraces, and, what Oliver wanted a great deal more, a piece of bread and butter, lest he should seem too hungry when he got to the workhouse. With the slice of bread in his hand, and the little brown-cloth parish cap upon his head, Oliver was then led away by Mr. Bumble from the wretched home where one kind word or look had never lighted the gloom of his infant years. And yet he burst into an agony of childish grief as the cottage-gate closed after him. Wretched as were the little companions in misery he was leaving behind, they were the only friends he had ever known; and a sense of his loneliness in the great wide world sank into the child's heart for the first time.

Mr. Bumble walked on with long strides, and little Oliver, firmly grasping his gold-laced cuff, trotted beside him, inquiring at the end of every quarter of a mile whether they were " nearly there," to which interrogations Mr. Bumble returned very brief and snappish replies; for the temporary blandness which gin and water awakens in some bosoms had by this time evaporated, and he was once again a beadle.

Oliver had not been within the walls of the workhouse a quarter of an hour, and had scarcely completed the demolition of a second slice of bread, when Mr. Bumble, who had handed him over to the care of an old woman, returned, and, telling him it was a board night, informed him that the board had said he was to appear before it forthwith.

Not having a very clearly defined notion of what a live board was, Oliver was rather astounded by this intelligence, and was not quite certain whether he ought to laugh or cry. He had no time to think about the matter, however; for Mr. Bumble gave him a tap on the head with his cane to wake him up, and another on the back to make him lively, and bidding him follow, conducted him into a large whitewashed room where eight or ten fat gentlemen were sitting round a table, at the top of which, seated in an arm-chair rather higher than the rest, was a particularly fat gentleman with a very round, red face.

"Bow to the board," said Bumble. Oliver brushed away two or three tears that were lingering in his eyes, and seeing no board but the table, fortunately bowed to that.

"What's your name, boy?" said the gentleman in the high chair.

Oliver was frightened at the sight of so many gentlemen, which made him tremble; and the beadle gave him another tap behind, which made him cry; and these two causes made him answer in a very low and hesitating voice; whereupon a gentleman in a white waistcoat said he was a fool, which was a capital way of raising his spirits, and putting him quite at his ease.

"Boy," said the gentleman in the high chair, "listen to me. You know you're an orphan, I suppose?"

"What's that, sir?" inquired poor Oliver.

"The boy *is* a fool—I thought he was," said the gentleman in the white waistcoat, in a very decided tone. If one member of a class be blessed with an intuitive perception of others of the same race, the gentleman in the white waistcoat was unquestionably well qualified to pronounce an opinion on the matter.

"Hush!" said the gentleman who had spoken first. "You know you've got no father or mother, and that you are brought up by the parish, don't you?"

"Yes, sir," replied Oliver, weeping bitterly.

"What are you crying for?" inquired the gentleman in the white waistcoat. And to be sure it was very extraordinary. What *could* the boy be crying for?

"I hope you say your prayers every night," said another gentleman in a gruff voice, "and pray for the people who feed you, and take care of you, like a Christian."

"Yes, sir," stammered the boy. The gentleman who spoke last was unconsciously right. It would have been *very* like a Christian, and a marvellously good Christian, too, if Oliver had prayed for the people who fed and took care of *him*. But he hadn't, because nobody had taught him.

"Well, you have come here to be educated, and taught a useful trade," said the red-faced gentleman in the high chair.

"So you'll begin to pick oakum to-morrow morning at six o'clock," added the surly one in the white waistcoat.

For the combination of both these blessings in the one simple process of picking oakum, Oliver bowed low by the direction of the beadle, and was then hurried away to a large ward, where, on a rough hard bed, he sobbed himself to sleep. What a noble illustration of the tender laws of this favoured country!—they let the paupers go to sleep!

Poor Oliver! He little thought, as he lay sleeping in happy unconsciousness of all around him, that the board had that very day arrived at a decision which would exercise the most material influence over all his future fortunes. But they had. And this was it:—

The members of this board were very sage, deep, philosophical men; and when they came to turn their attention to the workhouse, they found out at once, what ordinary folks would never have discovered—the poor people liked it! It was a regular place of public entertainment for the poorer classes—a tavern where there was nothing to pay—a public breakfast, dinner, tea, and supper all the year round—a brick and mortar elysium, where it was all play and no work. " Oho!" said the board, looking very knowing; " we are the fellows to set this to rights; we'll stop it all in no time." So, they established the rule, that all poor people should have the alternative (for they would compel nobody, not they,) of being starved by a gradual process in the house, or by a quick one out of it. With this view, they contracted with the water-works to lay on an unlimited supply of water, and with a corn-factor to supply periodically small quantities of oatmeal; and issued three meals of thin gruel a-day, with an onion twice a week, and half a roll on Sundays. They made a great many other wise and humane regulations having reference to the ladies, which it is not necessary to repeat; kindly undertook to divorce poor married people, in consequence of the great expense of a suit in Doctors' Commons; and, instead of compelling a man to support his family as they had theretofore done, took his family away from him, and made him a bachelor! There is no telling how many applicants for relief under these last two heads would not have started up in all classes of society, if it had not been coupled with the workhouse. But they were long-headed men, and they had provided for this difficulty. The relief was inseparable from the workhouse and the gruel, and that frightened the people.

For the first six months after Oliver Twist was removed, the system was in full operation. It was rather expensive at first, in consequence of the increase of the undertaker's bill, and the necessity of taking in the clothes of all the paupers, which fluttered loosely on their wasted, shrunken forms, after a week or two's gruel. But the number of workhouse inmates got thin as well as the paupers, and the board were in ecstasies.

The room in which the boys were fed was a large stone hall, with a copper at one end, out of which the master, dressed in an apron for the purpose, and assisted by one or two women, ladled the gruel at meal-times; of which composition each boy had one porringer, and no more—except on festive occasions, and then he had two ounces and a quarter of bread besides. The bowls never wanted washing— the boys polished them with their spoons till they shone again; and when they had performed this operation, (which never took very long, the spoons being nearly as large as the bowls,) they would sit staring at the copper with such eager eyes as if they could devour the very bricks of which it was composed; employing themselves meanwhile in sucking their fingers most assiduously, with the view of catching up any stray splashes of gruel that might have been cast thereon. Boys have generally excellent appetites. Oliver Twist and his companions suffered the tortures of slow starvation for three months; at last they got so voracious and wild with hunger, that one boy, who was tall for his age, and hadn't been used to that sort of thing, (for his father had kept a small cook's shop,) hinted darkly to his companions, that unless he had another basin of gruel *per diem*, he was afraid he should some night eat the boy who slept next him, who happened to be a weakly youth of tender age. He had a wild, hungry eye, and they implicitly believed him. A council was held; lots were cast who should walk up to the master after supper that evening, and ask for more; and it fell to Oliver Twist.

The evening arrived: the boys took their places; the master in his cook's uniform stationed himself at the copper; his pauper assistants ranged themselves behind him; the gruel was served out, and a long grace was said over the short commons. The gruel disappeared, and the boys whispered each other and winked at Oliver, while his next neighbours nudged him. Child as he was, he was desperate with

hunger and reckless with misery. He rose from the table, and advancing, basin and spoon in hand, to the master, said, somewhat alarmed at his own temerity—

"Please, sir, I want some more."

The master was a fat, healthy man, but he turned very pale. He gazed in stupefied astonishment on the small rebel for some seconds, and then clung for support to the copper. The assistants were paralysed with wonder, and the boys with fear.

"What!" said the master at length, in a faint voice.

"Please, sir," replied Oliver, "I want some more."

The master aimed a blow at Oliver's head with the ladle, pinioned him in his arms, and shrieked aloud for the beadle.

The board were sitting in solemn conclave when Mr. Bumble rushed into the room in great excitement, and addressing the gentleman in the high chair, said—

"Mr. Limbkins, I beg your pardon, sir;—Oliver Twist has asked for more." There was a general start. Horror was depicted on every countenance.

"For *more!*" said Mr. Limbkins. "Compose yourself, Bumble, and answer me distinctly. Do I understand that he asked for more, after he had eaten the supper allotted by the dietary?"

"He did, sir," replied Bumble.

"That boy will be hung," said the gentleman in the white waistcoat; "I know that boy will be hung."

Nobody controverted the prophetic gentleman's opinion. An animated discussion took place. Oliver was ordered into instant confinement; and a bill was next morning pasted on the outside of the gate, offering a reward of five pounds to anybody who would take Oliver Twist off the hands of the parish. In other words, five pounds and Oliver Twist were offered to any man or woman who wanted an apprentice to any trade, business or calling.

"I never was more convinced of anything in my life," said the gentleman in the white waistcoat, as he knocked at the gate and read the bill next morning—" I never was more convinced of anything in my life, than I am that that boy will come to be hung."

As I purpose to show in the sequel whether the white-waistcoated gentleman was right or not, I should perhaps mar the interest of this narrative (supposing it to possess any at all) if I ventured to hint just yet, whether the life of Oliver Twist had this violent termination or no.

CHAPTER III.

RELATES HOW OLIVER TWIST WAS VERY NEAR GETTING A PLACE, WHICH WOULD NOT HAVE BEEN A SINECURE.

For a week after the commission of the impious and profane offence of asking for more, Oliver remained a close prisoner in the dark and solitary room to which he had been consigned by the wisdom and mercy of the board. It appears, at first sight, not unreasonable to suppose, that, if he had entertained a becoming feeling of respect for the prediction of the gentleman in the white waistcoat, he would have established that sage individual's prophetic character, once and for ever, by tying one end of his pocket handkerchief to a hook in the wall, and attaching himself to the other. To the performance of this feat, however, there was one obstacle, namely, that pocket-handkerchiefs being decided articles of luxury, had been, for all future times and ages, removed from the noses of paupers by the express order of the board in council assembled, solemnly given and pronounced under their hands and seals. There was a still greater obstacle in Oliver's youth and childishness. He only cried bitterly all day; and when the long, dismal night came on, he spread his little hands before his eyes to shut out the darkness, and crouching in the corner, tried to sleep: ever and anon waking with a start and tremble, and drawing himself closer and closer to the wall, as if to feel even its cold hard surface were a protection in the gloom and loneliness which surrounded him.

Let it not be supposed by the enemies of "the system," that, during the period of his solitary incarceration, Oliver was denied the benefit of exercise, the pleasure of society, or the advantages of religious consolation. As for exercise, it was nice cold weather, and he was allowed to perform his ablutions every morning under the pump, in a stone yard, in the presence of Mr. Bumble, who prevented his catching cold, and caused a tingling sensation to pervade his frame, by repeated applications of the cane; as for society, he was carried every other day into the hall where the boys dined, and there sociably flogged as a public warning and example; and so far from being denied the advantages of religious consolation, he was kicked into the same apartment every evening at prayer-time, and there permitted to listen to, and console his mind with, a general supplication of the boys, containing a special clause therein inserted by authority of the board, in which they entreated to be made good, virtuous, contented, and obedient, and to be guarded from the sins and vices of Oliver Twist, whom the supplication distinctly set forth to be under the exclusive patronage and protection of the powers of wickedness, and an article direct from the manufactory of the devil himself.

It chanced one morning, while Oliver's affairs were in this auspicious and comfortable state, that Mr. Gamfield, chimney-sweeper, was wending his way adown the High-street, deeply cogitating in his mind his ways and means of paying certain arrears of rent, for which his landlord had become rather pressing. Mr. Gamfield's most sanguine calculation of funds could not raise them within full five pounds of the desired amount; and, in a species of arithmetical desperation, he was alternately cudgelling his brains and his donkey, when, passing the workhouse, his eyes encountered the bill on the gate.

"Wo—o!" said Mr. Gamfield to the donkey.

The donkey was in a state of profound abstraction,—wondering, probably, whether he was destined to be regaled with a cabbage-stalk or two, when he had disposed of the two sacks of soot with which the little cart was laden; so, without noticing the word of command, he jogged onwards.

Mr. Gamfield growled a fierce imprecation on the donkey generally, but more particularly on his eyes; and, running after him, bestowed a blow on his head, which would inevitably have beaten in any skull but a donkey's; then, catching hold of the bridle, he gave his jaw a sharp wrench, by way of gentle reminder that he was not his own master: and, having by these means turned him round, he gave him another blow on the head, just to stun him till he came back again; and having done so, walked up to the gate to read the bill.

The gentleman with the white waistcoat was standing at the gate with his hands behind him, after having delivered himself of some profound sentiments in the board-room. Having witnessed the little dispute between Mr. Gamfield and the donkey, he smiled joyously when that person came up to read the bill, for he saw at once that Mr. Gamfield was exactly the sort of master Oliver Twist wanted. Mr. Gamfield smiled, too, as he perused the document, for five pounds was just the sum he had been wishing for; and, as to the boy with which it was encumbered, Mr. Gamfield, knowing what the dietary of the workhouse was, well knew he would be a nice small pattern, just the very thing for register stoves. So he spelt the bill through again, from beginning to end, and then, touching his fur cap in token of humility, accosted the gentleman in the white waistcoat.

"This here boy, sir, wot the parish wants to 'prentis," said Mr. Gamfield.

"Yes, my man," said the gentleman in the white waistcoat, with a condescending smile, "what of him?"

"If the parish vould like him to learn a light pleasant trade, in a good 'spectable chimbley-sweepin' bisness," said Mr. Gamfield, " I wants a 'prentis, and I'm ready to take him."

"Walk in," said the gentleman in the white waistcoat. Mr. Gamfield having lingered behind, to give the donkey another blow on the head, and another wrench of the jaw, as a caution not to run away in his absence, followed the gentleman with the white waistcoat into the room where Oliver had first seen him.

"It's a nasty trade," said Mr. Limbkins when Gamfield had again stated his wish.

"Young boys have been smothered in chimneys before now," said another gentleman.

"That's acause they damped the straw afore they lit it in the chimbley to make 'em come down again," said Gamfield; "that's all smoke, and no blaze; vereas smoke ain't o' no use at all in makin' a boy come down, for it only sinds him to sleep, and that's wot he likes. Boys is wery obstinit, and wery lazy, gen'lmen, and there's nothink like a good hot blaze to make 'em com down vith a run; it's humane too, gen'lmen, acause, even if they've stuck in the chimbley, roastin' their feet makes 'em struggle to hextricate theirselves."

The gentleman in the white waistcoat appeared very much amused by this explanation; but his mirth was speedily checked by a look from Mr. Limbkins. The board then proceeded to converse among themselves for a few minutes, but in so low a tone, that the words " saving of expenditure," " look well in the accounts," " have a printed report published," were alone audible: and they only chanced to be heard on account of their being very frequently repeated with great emphasis.

At length the whispering ceased, and the members of the board having resumed their seats and their solemnity, Mr. Limbkins said,

" We have considered your proposition, and we don't approve of it."

"Not at all," said the gentleman in the white waistcoat.

"Decidedly not," added the other members.

As Mr. Gamfield did happen to labour under the slight imputation of having bruised three or four boys to death already, it occurred to him that the board had perhaps, in some unaccountable freak, taken it into their heads that this extraneous circumstance ought to influence their proceedings. It was very unlike their general mode of doing business, if they had; but still, as he had no particular wish to revive the rumour, he twisted his cap in his hands, and walked slowly from the table.

"So you won't let me have him, gen'lmen," said Mr. Gamfield, pausing near the door.

"No," replied Mr. Limbkins; "at least, as it's a nasty business, we think you ought to take something less than the premium we offered."

Mr. Gamfield's countenance brightened, as, with a quick step he returned to the table, and said,

"What'll you give, gen'lmen? Come, don't

be too hard on a poor man. What'll you give?"

"I should say three pound ten was plenty," said Mr. Limbkins.

"Ten shillings too much," said the gentleman in the white waistcoat.

"Come," said Gamfield; "say four pound, gen'lmen. Say four pound, and you've got rid of him for good and all. There!"

"Three pound ten," repeated Mr. Limbkins, firmly.

"Come, I'll split the difference, gen'lmen," urged Gamfield. "Three pound fifteen."

"Not a farthing more," was the firm reply of Mr. Limbkins.

"You're desp'rate hard upon me, gen'lmen," said Gamfield, wavering.

"Pooh! pooh! nonsense!" said the gentleman in the white waistcoat. "He'd be cheap with nothing at all, as a premium. Take him, you silly fellow! He's just the boy for you. He wants the stick now and then; it'll do him good; and his board needn't come very expensive, for he hasn't been overfed since he was born. Ha! ha! ha!"

Mr. Gamfield gave an arch look at the faces round the table, and, observing a smile on all of them, gradually broke into a smile himself. The bargain was made, and Mr. Bumble was at once instructed that Oliver Twist and his indentures were to be conveyed before the magistrate for signature and approval that very afternoon.

In pursuance of this determination, little Oliver, to his excessive astonishment, was released from bondage, and ordered to put himself into a clean shirt. He had hardly achieved this very unusual gymnastic performance, when Mr. Bumble brought him with his own hands a basin of gruel, and the holiday allowance of two ounces and a quarter of bread; at sight of which Oliver began to cry very piteously, thinking, not unnaturally, that the board must have determined to kill him for some useful purpose, or they never would have begun to fatten him up in this way.

"Don't make your eyes red, Oliver, but eat your food and be thankful," said Mr. Bumble, in a tone of impressive pomposity. "You're a-going to be made a 'prentice of, Oliver."

" A 'prentice, sir!" said the child, trembling.

" Yes, Oliver," said Mr. Bumble. " The kind and blessed gentlemen which is so many parents to you, Oliver, when you have none of your own, are a-going to 'prentice you, and to set you up in life, and make a man of you, although the expense to the parish is three pound ten!—three pound ten, Oliver!—seventy shillin's!—one hundred and forty sixpences!—and all for a naughty orphan which nobody can't love."

As Mr. Bumble paused to take breath after delivering this address in an awful voice, the tears rolled down the poor child's face, and he sobbed bitterly.

" Come," said Mr. Bumble, somewhat less pompously, for it was gratifying to his feelings to observe the effect his eloquence had produced, " come, Oliver, wipe your eyes with the cuffs of your jacket, and don't cry into your gruel; that's a very foolish action, Oliver." It certainly was, for there was quite enough water in it already.

On their way to the magistrates, Mr. Bumble instructed Oliver that all he would have to do, would be to look very happy, and say, when the gentleman asked him if he wanted to be apprenticed, that he should like it very much indeed; both of which injunctions Oliver promised to obey, the rather as Mr. Bumble threw in a gentle hint, that if he failed in either particular, there was no telling what would be done to him. When they arrived at the office, he was shut up in a little room by himself, and admonished by Mr. Bumble to stay there until he came back to fetch him.

There the boy remained with a palpitating heart for half an hour, at the expiration of which time Mr. Bumble thrust in his head, unadorned with the cocked hat, and said aloud,

"Now, Oliver, my dear, come to the gentleman." As Mr. Bumble said this, he put on a grim and threatening look, and added in a low voice, "Mind what I told you, you young rascal."

Oliver stared innocently in Mr. Bumble's face at this somewhat contradictory style of address; but that gentleman prevented his offering any remark thereupon, by leading him at once into an adjoining room, the door of which was open. It was a large room with a great window; and behind a desk sat two old gentlemen with powdered heads, one of whom was reading the newspaper, while the other was perusing, with the aid of a pair of tortoise-shell spectacles, a small piece of parchment which lay before him. Mr. Limbkins was standing in front of the desk on one side, and Mr. Gamfield, with a partially washed face, on the other, while two or three bluff-looking men in top-boots were lounging about.

The old gentleman with the spectacles gradually dozed off over the little bit of parchment, and there was a short pause, after Oliver had been stationed by Mr. Bumble in front of the desk.

"This is the boy, your worship," said Mr. Bumble.

The old gentleman who was reading the newspaper raised his head for a moment, and pulled the other old gentleman by the sleeve, whereupon the last-mentioned old gentleman woke up.

" Oh, is this the boy?" said the old gentleman.

" This is him, sir," replied Mr. Bumble. " Bow to the magistrate, my dear."

Oliver roused himself, and made his best obeisance. He had been wondering, with his eyes fixed on the magistrates' powder, whether all boards were born with that white stuff on their heads, and were boards from thenceforth on that account.

" Well," said the old gentleman, " I suppose he's fond of chimney-sweeping ?"

" He doats on it, your worship," replied Bumble, giving Oliver a sly pinch, to intimate that he had better not say he didn't.

" And he *will* be a sweep, will he? inquired the old gentleman.

" If we was to bind him to any other trade to-morrow, he'd run away simultaneously, your worship," replied Bumble.

" And this man that's to be his master— you, sir—you'll treat him well, and feed him, and do all that sort of thing,—will you?" said the old gentleman.

"When I says I will, I means I will," replied Mr. Gamfield doggedly.

"You're a rough speaker, my friend, but you look an honest, open-hearted man," said the old gentleman, turning his spectacles in the direction of the candidate for Oliver's premium, whose villanous countenance was a regular stamped receipt for cruelty. But the magistrate was half blind and half childish, so he couldn't reasonably be expected to discern what other people did.

"I hope I am, sir," said Mr. Gamfield with an ugly leer.

"I have no doubt you are, my friend," replied the old gentleman, fixing his spectacles more firmly on his nose, and looking about him for the inkstand.

It was the critical moment of Oliver's fate. If the inkstand had been where the old gentleman thought it was, he would have dipped his pen into it and signed the indentures, and Oliver would have been straightway hurried off. But as it chanced to be immediately under his nose, it followed as a matter of course that he looked all over his desk for it, without finding it; and happening in the course of his search to look straight before him, his gaze encountered the pale and terrified face of Oliver Twist, who, despite all the admonitory looks and pinches of Bumble, was regarding the very repulsive countenance of his future master with a mingled expression of horror and fear, too palpable to be mistaken even by a half-blind magistrate.

The old gentleman stopped, laid down his pen, and looked from Oliver to Mr. Limbkins, who attempted to take snuff with a cheerful and unconcerned aspect.

" My boy," said the old gentleman, leaning over the desk. Oliver started at the sound— he might be excused for doing so, for the words were kindly said, and strange sounds frighten one. He trembled violently, and burst into tears.

" My boy," said the old gentleman, " you look pale and alarmed. What is the matter?"

" Stand a little away from him, beadle," said the other magistrate, laying aside the paper, and leaning forward with an expression of interest. "Now, boy, tell us what's the matter: don't be afraid."

Oliver fell on his knees, and clasping his hands together, prayed that they would order him back to the dark room—that they would starve him—beat him—kill him if they pleased—rather than send him away with that dreadful man.

"Well!" said Mr. Bumble, raising his hands and eyes with most impressive solemnity,—"Well! of all the artful and designing orphans that ever I see, Oliver, you are one of the most bare-facedest."

"Hold your tongue, beadle," said the second old gentleman, when Mr. Bumble had given vent to this compound adjective.

"I beg your worship's pardon," said Mr. Bumble, incredulous of his having heard aright,—"did your worship speak to me?"

"Yes—hold your tongue."

Mr. Bumble was stupefied with astonishment. A beadle ordered to hold his tongue! A moral revolution!

The old gentleman in the tortoise-shell spectacles looked at his companion; he nodded significantly.

"We refuse to sanction these indentures," said the old gentleman, tossing aside the piece of parchment as he spoke.

"I hope," stammered Mr. Limbkins—" I hope the magistrates will not form the opinion that the authorities have been guilty of any improper conduct, on the unsupported testimony of a mere child."

"The magistrates are not called upon to pronounce any opinion on the matter," said the second old gentleman sharply. "Take the boy back to the workhouse, and treat him kindly. He seems to want it."

That same evening the gentleman in the white waistcoat most positively and decidedly affirmed, not only that Oliver would be hung, but that he would be drawn and quartered into the bargain. Mr. Bumble shook his head with gloomy mystery, and said he wished he might come to good; whereunto Mr. Gamfield replied, that he wished he might come to him, which, although he agreed with the beadle in most matters, would seem to be a wish of a totally opposite description.

The next morning the public were once more informed that Oliver Twist was again to let, and that five pounds would be paid to anybody who would take possession of him.

CHAPTER IV.

OLIVER, BEING OFFERED ANOTHER PLACE, MAKES HIS
FIRST ENTRY INTO PUBLIC LIFE.

IN great families, when an advantageous place cannot be obtained, either in possession, reversion, remainder, or expectancy, for the young man who is growing up, it is a very general custom to send him to sea. The board, in imitation of so wise and salutary an example, took counsel together on the expediency of shipping off Oliver Twist in some small trading vessel bound to a good unhealthy port, which suggested itself as the very best thing that could possibly be done with him; the probability being, that the skipper would either flog him to death in a playful mood some day after dinner, or knock his brains out with an iron bar—both pastimes being, as is pretty generally known, very favourite and common recreations among gentlemen of that class. The more the case presented itself to the board in this point of view, the more manifold the advantages of the step appeared; so they came to the conclusion, that the only way of providing for Oliver effectually, was to send him to sea without delay.

Mr. Bumble had been despatched to make various preliminary inquiries, with the view of finding out some captain or other who wanted a cabin-boy without any friends; and was returning to the workhouse to communicate the result of his mission, when he encountered just at the gate no less a person than Mr. Sowerberry, the parochial undertaker.

Mr. Sowerberry was a tall, gaunt, large-jointed man, attired in a suit of thread-bare black, with darned cotton stockings of the same colour, and shoes to answer. His features were not naturally intended to wear a smiling aspect, but he was in general rather given to professional jocosity; his step was elastic, and his face betokened inward pleasantry, as he advanced to Mr. Bumble and shook him cordially by the hand.

"I have taken the measure of the two women that died last night, Mr. Bumble," said the undertaker.

"You'll make your fortune, Mr. Sowerberry," said the beadle, as he thrust his thumb and forefinger into the proffered snuff-box of the undertaker, which was an ingenious little model of a patent coffin. "I say you'll make your fortune, Mr. Sowerberry," repeated Mr. Bumble, tapping the undertaker on the shoulder in a friendly manner with his cane.

"Think so?" said the undertaker in a tone which half admitted and half disputed the probability of the event. "The prices allowed by the board are very small, Mr. Bumble."

"So are the coffins," replied the beadle, with precisely as near an approach to a laugh as a great official ought to indulge in.

Mr. Sowerberry was much tickled at this, as of course he ought to be, and laughed a long time without cessation. "Well, well, Mr. Bumble," he said at length, "there's no denying that, since the new system of feeding has come in, the coffins are something narrower and more shallow than they used to be; but we must have some profit, Mr. Bumble. Well-seasoned timber is an expensive article, sir; and all the iron handles come by canal from Birmingham."

"Well, well," said Mr. Bumble, "every trade has its drawbacks, and a fair profit is of course allowable."

"Of course, of course," replied the undertaker; "and if I don't get a profit upon this or that particular article, why, I make it up in the long-run, you see—he! he! he!"

"Just so," said Mr. Bumble.

"Though I must say,"—continued the undertaker, resuming the current of observations which the beadle had interrupted—"though I must say, Mr. Bumble, that I have to contend against one very great disadvantage, which is, that all the stout people go off the quickest— I mean that the people who have been better off, and have paid rates for many years, are the first to sink when they come into the house: and let me tell you, Mr. Bumble, that three or four inches over one's calculation makes a great hole in one's profits, especially when one has a family to provide for, sir."

As Mr. Sowerberry said this, with the becoming indignation of an ill-used man, and as Mr. Bumble felt that it rather tended to convey a reflection on the honour of the parish, the latter gentleman thought it advisable to change the subject; and Oliver Twist being uppermost in his mind, he made him his theme.

"By the bye," said Mr. Bumble, " you don't know anybody who wants a boy, do you —a porochial 'prentis, who is at present a dead-weight—a millstone, as I may say—round the porochial throat? Liberal terms, Mr. Sowerberry—liberal terms;"—and, as Mr. Bumble spoke, he raised his cane to the bill above him, and gave three distinct raps upon the words " five pounds," which were printed thereon in Roman capitals of gigantic size.

" Gadso!" said the undertaker, taking Mr. Bumble by the gilt-edged lappel of his official coat; " that's just the very thing I wanted to speak to you about. You know—dear me, what a very elegant button this is, Mr. Bumble; I never noticed it before."

"Yes, I think it is rather pretty," said the beadle, glancing proudly downwards at the large brass buttons which embellished his coat. "The die is the same as the porochial seal—the Good Samaritan healing the sick and bruised man. The board presented it to me on New-year's morning, Mr Sowerberry. I put it on, I remember, for the first time, to attend the inquest on that reduced tradesman who died in a doorway at midnight."

"I recollect," said the undertaker. "The jury brought in, 'Died from exposure to the cold, and want of the common necessaries of life,'—didn't they?"

Mr. Bumble nodded.

"And they made it a special verdict, I think," said the undertaker, "by adding some words to the effect, that if the relieving officer had ——"

"Tush—foolery!" interposed the beadle angrily. "If the board attended to all the nonsense that ignorant jurymen talk, they'd have enough to do."

" Very true," said the undertaker; " they would indeed."

" Juries," said Mr. Bumble, grasping his cane tightly, as was his wont when working into a passion—" juries is ineddicated, vulgar, grovelling wretches."

" So they are," said the undertaker.

" They haven't no more philosophy nor political economy about 'em than that," said the beadle, snapping his fingers contemptuously.

" No more they have," acquiesced the undertaker.

" I despise 'em," said the beadle, growing very red in the face.

" So do I," rejoined the undertaker.

" And I only wish we 'd a jury of the independent sort in the house for a week or two," said the beadle; " the rules and regulations of the board would soon bring their spirit down for them."

" Let 'em alone for that," replied the undertaker. So saying, he smiled approvingly to calm the rising wrath of the indignant parish officer.

Mr. Bumble lifted off his cocked hat, took a handkerchief from the inside of the crown, wiped from his forehead the perspiration which his rage had engendered, fixed the cocked hat on again; and, turning to the undertaker, said in a calmer voice,

"Well; what about the boy?"

"Oh!" replied the undertaker; "why, you know, Mr. Bumble, I pay a good deal towards the poor's rates."

"Hem!" said Mr. Bumble. "Well?"

"Well," replied the undertaker, "I was thinking that if I pay so much towards 'em, I've a right to get as much out of 'em as I can, Mr. Bumble; and so—and so—I think I'll take the boy myself."

Mr. Bumble grasped the undertaker by the arm, and led him into the building. Mr. Sowerberry was closeted with the board for five minutes, and it was arranged that Oliver should go to him that evening " upon liking,"

—a phrase which means, in the case of a parish apprentice, that if the master find, upon a short trial, that he can get enough work out of a boy without putting too much food in him, he shall have him for a term of years, to do what he likes with.

When little Oliver was taken before " the gentlemen " that evening, and informed that he was to go that night as general house-lad to a coffin-maker's, and that if he complained of his situation, or ever came back to the parish again, he would be sent to sea, there to be drowned, or knocked on the head, as the case might be, he evinced so little emotion, that they by common consent pronounced him a hardened young rascal, and ordered Mr. Bumble to remove him forthwith.

Now, although it was very natural that the board, of all people in the world, should feel in a great state of virtuous astonishment and horror at the smallest tokens of want of feeling on the part of anybody, they were rather out in this particular instance. The simple fact was, that Oliver, instead of possessing too little feeling, possessed rather too much, and was in a fair way of being reduced to a state of brutal stupidity and sullenness for life by the ill usage he had received. He heard the news of his destination in perfect silence, and, having had his luggage put into his hand—which was not very difficult to carry, inasmuch as it was all comprised within the limits of a brown paper parcel, about half a foot square by three inches deep—he pulled his cap over his eyes, and once more attaching himself to Mr. Bumble's coat cuff, was led away by that dignitary to a new scene of suffering.

For some time Mr. Bumble drew Oliver along without notice or remark, for the beadle carried his head very erect, as a beadle always should; and, it being a windy day, little Oliver was completely enshrouded by the skirts of Mr. Bumble's coat as they blew open, and disclosed to great advantage his flapped waistcoat and drab plush knee-breeches. As they drew near to their destination, however, Mr. Bumble thought it expedient to look down and see that the boy was in good order for inspection by his new master, which he accordingly did, with a fit and becoming air of gracious patronage.

" Oliver !" said Mr. Bumble.

" Yes, sir," replied Oliver, in a low, tremulous voice.

" Pull that cap off your eyes, and hold up your head, sir."

Although Oliver did as he was desired at once, and passed the back of his unoccupied hand briskly across his eyes, he left a tear in them when he looked up at his conductor. As Mr. Bumble gazed sternly upon him, it rolled down his cheek. It was followed by another, and another. The child made a strong effort, but it was an unsuccessful one; and, withdrawing his other hand from Mr. Bumble's, he covered his face with both, and wept till the tears sprung out from between his thin and bony fingers.

" Well!" exclaimed Mr. Bumble, stopping short, and darting at his little charge a look of intense malignity,—" well, of *all* the ungratefullest and worst-disposed boys as ever I see, Oliver, you are the——"

" No, no, sir," sobbed Oliver, clinging to the hand which held the well-known cane; " no, no, sir; I will be good indeed; indeed, indeed I will, sir! I am a very little boy, sir, ; and it is so—so—"

" So what?" inquired Mr. Bumble in amazement.

" So lonely, sir—so very lonely," cried the child. " Everybody hates me. Oh! sir, don't, don't pray be cross to me." The child beat his hand upon his heart, and looked into his companion's face with tears of real agony.

Mr. Bumble regarded Oliver's piteous and helpless look with some astonishment for a few seconds, hemmed three or four times in a husky manner, and, after muttering something about " that troublesome cough," bid Oliver dry his eyes and be a good boy; and, once more taking his hand, walked on with him in silence.

The undertaker had just put up the shutters of his shop, and was making some entries in his day-book by the light of a most appropriately dismal candle, when Mr. Bumble entered.

" Aha!" said the undertaker, looking up from the book, and pausing in the middle of a word; " is that you, Bumble?"

" No one else, Mr. Sowerberry," replied the beadle. " Here, I've brought the boy." Oliver made a bow.

" Oh! that's the boy, is it?" said the undertaker, raising the candle above his head to get a full glimpse of Oliver. " Mrs. Sowerberry! will you come here a moment, my dear?"

Mrs. Sowerberry emerged from a little room behind the shop, and presented the form of a short, thin, squeezed-up woman, with a vixenish countenance.

" My dear," said Mr. Sowerberry, deferentially, " this is the boy from the workhouse that I told you of." Oliver bowed again.

" Dear me!" said the undertaker's wife, " he's very small."

" Why, he *is* rather small," replied Mr. Bumble, looking at Oliver as if it were his fault that he was no bigger; " he *is* small,—there's no denying it. But he'll grow, Mrs. Sowerberry,—he'll grow."

"Ah! I dare say he will," replied the lady pettishly, "on our victuals and our drink. I see no saving in parish children, not I; for they always cost more to keep than they're worth: however, men always think they know best. There, get down stairs, little bag o' bones." With this, the undertaker's wife opened a side door, and pushed Oliver down a steep flight of stairs into a stone cell, damp and dark, forming the ante-room to the coal-cellar, and denominated " the kitchen," wherein sat a slatternly girl in shoes down at heel, and blue worsted stockings very much out of repair.

"Here, Charlotte," said Mrs. Sowerberry, who had followed Oliver down, "give this boy some of the cold bits that were put by for Trip: he hasn't come home since the morning, so he may go without 'em. I dare say he isn't too dainty to eat 'em,—are you, boy?"

Oliver, whose eyes had glistened at the mention of meat, and who was trembling with eagerness to devour it, replied in the negative and a plateful of coarse broken victuals was set before him.

I wish some well-fed philosopher, whose meat and drink turn to gall within him, whose blood is ice, and whose heart is iron, could have seen Oliver Twist clutching at the dainty viands that the dog had neglected, and witnessed the horrible avidity with which he tore the bits asunder with all the ferocity of famine: —there is only one thing I should like better, and that would be to see him making the same sort of meal himself, with the same relish.

"Well," said the undertaker's wife, when Oliver had finished his supper, which she had regarded in silent horror, and with fearful auguries of his future appetite, "have you done?"

There being nothing eatable within his reach, Oliver replied in the affirmative.

"Then come with me," said Mrs. Sowerberry, taking up a dim and dirty lamp, and leading the way up stairs; "your bed's under the counter. You won't mind sleeping among the coffins, I suppose?—but it doesn't much matter whether you will or not, for you won't sleep anywhere else. Come; don't keep me here all night."

Oliver lingered no longer, but meekly followed his new mistress.

CHAPTER V.

OLIVER MINGLES WITH NEW ASSOCIATES, AND, GOING TO A FUNERAL FOR THE FIRST TIME, FORMS AN UNFAVOURABLE NOTION OF HIS MASTER'S BUSINESS.

Oliver, being left to himself in the undertaker's shop, set the lamp down on a workman's bench, and gazed timidly about him with a feeling of awe and dread, which many people a good deal older than he was will be at no loss to understand. An unfinished coffin on black tressels, which stood in the middle of the shop, looked so gloomy and death-like that a cold tremble came over him every time his eyes wandered in the direction of the dismal object, from which he almost expected to see some frightful form slowly rear its head to drive him mad with terror. Against the wall were ranged in regular array a long row of elm boards cut into the same shape, and looking in the dim light like high-shouldered ghosts with their hands in their breeches-pockets. Coffin-plates, elm chips, bright-headed nails, and shreds of black cloth, lay scattered on the floor; and the wall behind the counter was ornamented with a lively representation of two mutes in very stiff neckcloths, on duty at a large private door, with a hearse drawn by four black steeds approaching in the distance. The shop was close and hot, and the atmosphere seemed tainted with the smell of coffins. The recess beneath the counter in which his flock mattress was thrust, looked like a grave.

Nor were these the only dismal feelings which depressed Oliver. He was alone in a strange place; and we all know how chilled and desolate the best of us will sometimes feel in such a situation. The boy had no friends to care for, or to care for him. The regret of no recent separation was fresh in his mind; the absence of no loved and well-remembered face sunk heavily into his heart. But his heart *was* heavy, notwithstanding; and he wished, as he crept into his narrow bed, that that were his coffin, and that he could be laid in a calm and lasting sleep in the churchyard ground, with the tall grass waving gently above his head, and the sound of the old deep bell to soothe him in his sleep.

Oliver was awakened in the morning by a loud kicking at the outside of the shop-door, which, before he could huddle on his clothes, was repeated in an angry and impetuous manner about twenty-five times; and, when he began to undo the chain, the legs left off their volleys, and a voice began.

" Open the door, will yer?" cried the voice which belonged to the legs which had kicked at the door.

" I will, directly, sir," replied Oliver, undoing the chain, and turning the key.

" I suppose yer the new boy, a'n't yer?" said the voice, through the key-hole.

" Yes, sir," replied Oliver.

" How old are yer?" inquired the voice.

" Ten, sir," replied Oliver.

" Then I'll whop yer when I get in," said

the voice; "you just see if I don't, that's all, my work'us brat!" and having made this obliging promise, the voice began to whistle.

Oliver had been too often subjected to the process to which the very expressive monosyllable just recorded, bears reference, to entertain the smallest doubt that the owner of the voice, whoever he might be, would redeem his pledge most honourably. He drew back the bolts with a trembling hand, and opened the door.

For a second or two Oliver glanced up the street, and down the street, and over the way, impressed with the belief that the unknown, who had addressed him through the key-hole, had walked a few paces off to warm himself, for nobody did he see but a big charity-boy sitting on a post in front of the house, eating a slice of bread and butter, which he cut into wedges, the size of his mouth, with a clasp-knife, and then consumed with great dexterity.

"I beg your pardon, sir," said Oliver, at length: seeing that no other visitor made his appearance; "did you knock?"

"I kicked," replied the charity-boy.

"Did you want a coffin, sir?" inquired Oliver, innocently.

At this the charity-boy looked monstrous fierce, and said that Oliver would stand in need of one before long, if he cut jokes with his superiors in that way.

"Yer don't know who I am, I suppose, Work'us?" said the charity-boy, in continuation; descending from the top of the post, meanwhile, with edifying gravity.

"No sir," rejoined Oliver.

"I'm Mister Noah Claypole," said the charity-boy, "and you're under me. Take down the shutters, yer idle young ruffian!" With this, Mr. Claypole administered a kick to Oliver, and entered the shop with a dignified air, which did him great credit. It is difficult for a large-headed, small-eyed youth, of lumbering make and heavy countenance, to look dignified under any circumstances; but it is more especially so, when superadded to these personal attractions are a red nose and yellow smalls."

Oliver having taken down the shutters, and broken a pane of glass in his efforts to stagger away beneath the weight of the first one to a small court at the side of the house in which they were kept during the day, was graciously assisted by Noah, who, having consoled him with the assurance that " he'd catch it," condescended to help him. Mr. Sowerberry came down soon after, and, shortly afterwards, Mrs Sowerberry appeared; and Oliver having "caught it," in fulfilment of Noah's prediction, followed that young gentleman down stairs to breakfast.

" Come near the fire, Noah," said Charlotte. " I saved a nice little piece of bacon for you from master's breakfast. Oliver, shut that door at Mister Noah's back, and take them bits that I've put out on the cover of the bread-pan. There's your tea; take it away to that box, and drink it there, and make haste, for they'll want you to mind the shop. D'ye hear?"

" D'ye hear, Work'us?" said Noah Claypole.

" Lor, Noah!" said Charlotte, " what a rum creature you are! Why don't you let the boy alone?"

" Let him alone!" said Noah. " Why

every body lets him alone enough, for the matter of that. Neither his father nor mother will ever interfere with him: all his relations let him have his own way pretty well. Eh, Charlotte? He! he! he!"

"Oh, you queer soul!" said Charlotte, bursting into a hearty laugh, in which she was joined by Noah; after which they both looked scornfully at poor Oliver Twist, as he sat shivering upon the box in the coldest corner of the room, and ate the stale pieces which had been specially reserved for him.

Noah was a charity-boy, but not a workhouse orphan. No chance-child was he, for he could trace his genealogy all the way back to his parents, who lived hard by; his mother being a washerwoman, and his father a drunken soldier, discharged with a wooden leg and a diurnal pension of twopence-halfpenny and an unstateable fraction. The shop-boys in the neighbourhood had long been in the habit of branding Noah in the public streets with the ignominious epithets of "leathers," "charity," and the like; and Noah had borne them without reply. But now that fortune had cast in his way a nameless orphan, at whom even the meanest could point the finger of scorn, he retorted on him with interest. This affords charming food for contemplation. It shows us what a beautiful thing human nature sometimes is, and how impartially the same amiable qualities are developed in the finest lord and the dirtiest charity-boy.

Oliver had been sojourning at the undertaker's some three weeks or a month, and Mr. and Mrs. Sowerberry, the shop being shut up, were taking their supper in the little back-parlour, when Mr. Sowerberry, after several deferential glances at his wife, said,

" My dear—" He was going to say more; but, Mrs. Sowerberry looking up with a peculiarly unpropitious aspect, he stopped short.

" Well," said Mrs. Sowerberry, sharply.

" Nothing, my dear, nothing," said Mr. Sowerberry.

" Ugh, you brute !" said Mrs. Sowerberry.

" Not at all, my dear," said Mr. Sowerberry

humbly. "I thought you didn't want to hear, my dear. I was only going to say——"

"Oh, don't tell me what you were going to say," interposed Mrs. Sowerberry. "I am nobody; don't consult me, pray. *I* don't want to intrude upon your secrets." And, as Mrs. Sowerberry said this, she gave an hysterical laugh, which threatened violent consequences.

"But, my dear," said Sowerberry, "I want to ask your advice."

"No, no, don't ask mine," replied Mrs. Sowerberry, in an affecting manner: "ask somebody else's." Here there was another hysterical laugh, which frightened Mr. Sowerberry very much. This is a very common and much-approved matrimonial course of treatment, which is often very effective. It at once reduced Mr. Sowerberry to begging as a special favour to be allowed to say what Mrs. Sowerberry was most curious to hear, and, after a short altercation of less than three quarters of an hour's duration, the permission was most graciously conceded.

E 2

"It's only about young Twist, my dear," said Mr. Sowerberry. "A very good-looking boy that, my dear."

"He need be, for he eats enough," observed the lady.

"There's an expression of melancholy in his face, my dear," resumed Mr. Sowerberry, "which is very interesting. He would make a delightful mute, my dear."

Mrs. Sowerberry looked up with an expression of considerable wonderment. Mr. Sowerberry remarked it, and, without allowing time for any observation on the good lady's part, proceeded.

"I don't mean a regular mute to attend grown-up people, my dear, but only for children's practice. It would be very new to have a mute in proportion, my dear. You may depend upon it that it would have a superb effect."

Mrs. Sowerberry, who had a good deal of taste in the undertaking way, was much struck by the novelty of this idea; but, as it would have been compromising her dignity to have said so under existing circumstances, she merely inquired with much sharpness why such an obvious suggestion had not presented itself to her husband's mind before. Mr. Sowerberry rightly construed this as an acquiescence in his proposition; it was speedily determined that Oliver should be at once initiated into the mysteries of the profession, and, with this view, that he should accompany his master on the very next occasion of his services being required.

The occasion was not long in coming; for, half an hour after breakfast next morning, Mr. Bumble entered the shop, and supporting his cane against the counter, drew forth his large leathern pocket-book, from which he selected a small scrap of paper, which he handed over to Sowerberry.

"Aha!" said the undertaker, glancing over it with a lively countenance; "an order for a coffin, eh?"

"For a coffin first, and a porochial funeral afterwards," replied Mr. Bumble, fastening the strap of the leathern pocket-book, which, like himself, was very corpulent.

"Bayton," said the undertaker, looking from the scrap of paper to Mr. Bumble; "I never heard the name before."

Bumble shook his head as he replied, "Obstinate people, Mr. Sowerberry, very obstinate; proud, too, I'm afraid, sir."

"Proud, eh?" exclaimed Mr. Sowerberry with a sneer.—"Come, that's too much."

"Oh, it's sickening," replied the beadle; "perfectly antimonial, Mr. Sowerberry."

"So it is," acquiesced the undertaker.

"We only heard of them the night before last," said the beadle; "and we shouldn't have known anything about them then, only a woman who lodges in the same house made an application to the porochial committee for them to send the porochial surgeon to see a woman as was very bad. He had gone out to dinner; but his 'prentice, which is a very clever lad, sent 'em some medicine in a blacking-bottle, off-hand."

"Ah, there's promptness," said the undertaker.

"Promptness, indeed!" replied the beadle.

"But what's the consequence; what's the ungrateful behaviour of these rebels, sir? Why, the husband sends back word that the medicine won't suit his wife's complaint, and so she shan't take it—says she shan't take it, sir. Good, strong, wholesome medicine, as was given with great success to two Irish labourers and a coalheaver only a week before—sent 'em for nothing, with a blackin-bottle in,—and he sends back word that she shan't take it, sir."

As the flagrant atrocity presented itself to Mr. Bumble's mind in full force, he struck the counter sharply with his cane, and became flushed with indignation.

"Well," said the undertaker, "I ne—ver—did——"

"Never did, sir!" ejaculated the beadle,— "no, nor nobody never did; but, now she's— dead, we've got to bury her, and that's the direction, and the sooner it's done the better."

Thus saying, Mr. Bumble put on his cocked hat wrong side first, in a fever of parochial excitement, and flounced out of the shop.

"Why, he was so angry, Oliver, that he forgot even to ask after you," said Mr. Sowerberry, looking after the beadle as he strode down the street.

"Yes, sir," replied Oliver, who had carefully kept himself out of sight during the interview, and who was shaking from head to foot at the mere recollection of the sound of Mr. Bumble's voice. He needn't have taken the trouble to shrink from Mr. Bumble's glance, however; for that functionary, on whom the prediction of the gentleman in the white waistcoat had made a very strong impression, thought that now the undertaker had got Oliver upon trial, the subject was better avoided, until such time as he should be firmly bound for seven years, and all danger of his being returned upon the hands of the parish should be thus effectually and legally overcome.

"Well," said Mr. Sowerberry, taking up his hat, "the sooner this job is done the better. Noah, look after the shop. Oliver, put on your cap, and come with me." Oliver obeyed, and followed his master on his professional mission.

They walked on for some time through the

most crowded and densely inhabited part of the town, and then striking down a narrow street more dirty and miserable than any they had yet passed through, paused to look for the house which was the object of their search. The houses on either side were high and large, but very old, and tenanted by people of the poorest class, as their neglected appearance would have sufficiently denoted without the concurrent testimony afforded by the squalid looks of the few men and women who, with folded arms and bodies half doubled, occasionally skulked along. A great many of the tenements had shop-fronts; but they were fast closed, and mouldering away: only the upper rooms being inhabited. Others which had become insecure from age and decay, were prevented from falling into the street by huge beams of wood which were reared against the walls, and firmly planted in the road; but even these crazy dens seemed to have been selected as the nightly haunts of some houseless wretches, for many of the rough boards which supplied the place of door and window were wrenched from their positions to afford an aperture wide enough for the passage of a human body. The kennel was stagnant and filthy; the very rats which here and there lay putrefying in its rottenness, were hideous with famine.

There was neither knocker nor bell-handle at the open door where Oliver and his master stopped; so, groping his way cautiously through the dark passage, and bidding Oliver keep close to him and not be afraid, the undertaker mounted to the top of the first flight of stairs, and stumbling against a door on the landing, rapped at it with his knuckles.

It was opened by a young girl of thirteen or fourteen. The undertaker at once saw enough of what the room contained, to know it was the apartment to which he had been directed. He stepped in, and Oliver followed him.

There was no fire in the room; but a man was crouching mechanically over the empty stove. An old woman, too had drawn a low stool to the cold hearth, and was sitting beside him. There were some ragged children in another corner; and in a small recess opposite

the door there lay upon the ground something
covered with an old blanket. Oliver shuddered
as he cast his eyes towards the place, and
crept involuntarily closer to his master; for
though it was covered up, the boy *felt* that it
was a corpse.

The man's face was thin and very pale; his
hair and beard were grizzly, and his eyes were
bloodshot. The old woman's face was wrinkled;
her two remaining teeth protruded over her
under lip, and her eyes were bright and pier-
cing. Oliver was afraid to look at either her
or the man,—they seemed so like the rats he
had seen outside.

" Nobody shall go near her," said the man,
starting fiercely up, as the undertaker approached the recess. " Keep back! d—n you, keep
back, if you 've a life to lose."

" Nonsense! my good man," said the undertaker, who was pretty well used to misery in
all its shapes,—" nonsense!"

" I tell you," said the man, clenching his
hands, and stamping furiously on the floor,—
" I tell you I won't have her put into the

ground. She couldn't rest there. The worms would worry—not eat her,—she is so worn away."

The undertaker offered no reply to this raving, but producing a tape from his pocket, knelt down for a moment by the side of the body.

"Ah!" said the man, bursting into tears, and sinking on his knees at the feet of the dead woman; "kneel down, kneel down—kneel round her every one of you, and mark my words. I say she was starved to death. I never knew how bad she was till the fever came upon her, and then her bones were starting through the skin. There was neither fire nor candle; she died in the dark—in the dark. She couldn't even see her children's faces, though we heard her gasping out their names. I begged for her in the streets, and they sent me to prison. When I came back, she was dying; and all the blood in my heart has dried up, for they starved her to death. I swear it before the God that saw it,—they starved her!"—He twined his hands in his hair, and with a loud scream rolled grovelling upon the floor, his eyes fixed, and the foam gushing from his lips.

The terrified children cried bitterly; but the old woman, who had hitherto remained as quiet as if she had been wholly deaf to all that passed, menaced them into silence, and having unloosened the man's cravat, who still remained extended on the ground, tottered towards the undertaker.

"She was my daughter," said the old woman, nodding her head in the direction of the corpse, and speaking with an idiotic leer, more ghastly than even the presence of death itself.—"Lord, Lord!—well, it *is* strange that I who gave birth to her, and was a woman then, should be alive and merry now, and she lying there so cold and stiff! Lord, Lord!—to think of it;—it's as good as a play—as good as a play!"

As the wretched creature mumbled and chuckled in her hideous merriment, the undertaker turned to go away.

"Stop, stop!" said the old woman in a loud whisper. "Will she be buried to-morrow—or next day—or to-night? I laid her out, and I must walk, you know. Send me a large cloak —a good warm one, for it is bitter cold. We should have cake and wine, too, before we go! Never mind: send some bread—only a loaf of bread and a cup of water. Shall we have some bread, dear?" she said eagerly, catching at the undertaker's coat, as he once more moved towards the door.

"Yes, yes," said the undertaker, "of course; anything, everything." He disengaged himself from the old woman's grasp, and, dragging Oliver after him, hurried away.

The next day, (the family having been meanwhile relieved with a half-quartern loaf and a piece of cheese, left with them by Mr. Bumble himself,) Oliver and his master returned to the miserable abode, where Mr. Bumble had already arrived, accompanied by four men from the workhouse, who were to act as bearers. An old black cloak had been thrown over the rags of the old woman and the man: and the bare coffin having been screwed down, was hoisted on the shoulders of the bearers, and carried into the street.

"Now, you must put your best leg foremost, old lady," whispered Sowerberry in the old woman's ear; "we are rather late, and it won't do to keep the clergyman waiting Move on, my men,—as quick as you like."

Thus directed, the bearers trotted on under their light burden, and the two mourners kept as near them as they could. Mr. Bumble and Sowerberry walked at a good smart pace in front; and Oliver, whose legs were not so long as his master's, ran by the side.

There was not so great a necessity for hurrying as Mr. Sowerberry had anticipated, however; for when they reached the obscure corner of the churchyard in which the nettles grew, and the parish graves were made, the clergyman had not arrived, and the clerk, who was sitting by the vestry-room fire, seemed to think it by no means improbable that it might be an hour or so before he came. So they put the bier down on the brink of the grave; and the two mourners waited patiently in the damp clay with a cold rain drizzling down, while the ragged boys, whom the spectacle had attracted into the churchyard, played a noisy game at hide-and-seek among the tomb-stones, or varied their amusements by jumping backwards and forwards over the coffin. Mr. Sowerberry and Bumble, being personal friends of the clerk, sat by the fire with him, and read the paper.

At length, after the lapse of something more than an hour, Mr. Bumble, and Sowerberry, and the clerk, were seen running towards the grave; and immediately afterwards the clergyman appeared, putting on his surplice as he came along. Mr. Bumble then threshed a boy or two, to keep up appearances; and the reverend gentleman, having read as much of the burial service as could be compressed into four minutes, gave his surplice to the clerk, and ran away again.

"Now, Bill," said Sowerberry to the grave-digger, "fill up."

It was no very difficult task, for the grave was so full that the uppermost coffin was within a few feet of the surface. The grave-digger shovelled in the earth, stamped it loosely down with his feet, shouldered his spade, and walked off, followed by the boys, who murmured very loud complaints at the fun being over so soon.

"Come, my good fellow," said Bumble, tapping the man on the back, "they want to shut up the yard."

The man, who had never once moved since he had taken his station by the grave side, started, raised his head, stared at the person who had addressed him, walked forward for a few paces, and fell down in a swoon. The crazy old woman was too much occupied in bewailing the loss of her cloak (which the undertaker had taken off) to pay him any attention; so they threw a can of cold water over him, and when he came to, saw him safely out of the churchyard, locked the gate, and departed on their different ways.

"Well, Oliver," said Sowerberry, as they walked home, "how do you like it?"

"Pretty well, thank you, sir," replied Oliver, with considerable hesitation. "Not very much, sir."

"Ah, you'll get used to it in time, Oliver,"

said Sowerberry. " Nothing when you *are* used to it, my boy."

Oliver wondered in his own mind whether it had taken a very long time to get Mr. Sowerberry used to it; but he thought it better not to ask the question, and walked back to the shop, thinking over all he had seen and heard.

CHAPTER VI.

OLIVER, BEING GOADED BY THE TAUNTS OF NOAH, ROUSES
INTO ACTION, AND RATHER ASTONISHES HIM.

THE month's trial over, Oliver was formally apprenticed. It was a nice sickly season just at this time. In commercial phrase, coffins were looking up; and, in the course of a few weeks, Oliver had acquired a great deal of experience. The success of Mr. Sowerberry's ingenious speculation exceeded even his most sanguine hopes. The oldest inhabitants recollected no period at which measles had been so prevalent, or so fatal to infant existence; and many were the mournful processions which little Oliver headed in a hat-band reaching down to his knees, to the indescribable admiration and emotion of all the mothers in the town. As Oliver accompanied his master in most of his adult expeditions too, in order that he might acquire that unanimity of demeanour and full command of nerve which are so essential to a finished undertaker, he had many opportunities of observing the beautiful resignation and fortitude with which some strong-minded people bear their trials and losses.

For instance, when Sowerberry had an order for the burial of some rich old lady or gentleman, who was surrounded by a great number of nephews and nieces, who had been perfectly inconsolable during the previous illness, and whose grief had been wholly irrepressible even on the most public occasions, they would be as happy among themselves as need be—quite cheerful and contented, conversing together with as much freedom and gaiety as if nothing whatever had happened to disturb them. Husbands, too, bore the loss of their wives with the most heroic calmness; and wives, again, put on weeds for their husbands, as if, so far from grieving in the garb of sorrow, they had made up their minds to render it as becoming and attractive as possible. It was observable, too, that ladies and gentlemen who were in passions of anguish during the ceremony of interment, recovered almost as soon as they reached home, and became quite composed before the tea-drinking was over. All this was very pleasant and improving to see, and Oliver beheld it with great admiration.

That Oliver Twist was moved to resignation by the example of these good people, I cannot, although I am his biographer, undertake to affirm with any degree of confidence; but I can most distinctly say, that for many months he continued meekly to submit to the domination and ill-treatment of Noah Claypole, who used him far worse than ever, now that his jealousy was roused by seeing the new boy promoted to the black stick and hat-band, while he, the old one, remained stationary in the muffin-cap and leathers. Charlotte treated him badly because Noah did; and Mrs. Sowerberry was his decided enemy because Mr. Sowerberry was disposed to be his friend: so, between these three on one side, and a glut of funerals on the other, Oliver was not altogether as comfortable as the hungry pig was, when he was shut up by mistake in the grain department of a brewery.

And now I come to a very important passage in Oliver's history, for I have to record an act, slight and unimportant perhaps in appearance, but which indirectly produced a most material change in all his future prospects and proceedings.

One day Oliver and Noah had descended into the kitchen, at the usual dinner-hour, to banquet upon a small joint of mutton—a pound and a half of the worst end of the neck; when, Charlotte being called out of the way, there ensued a brief interval of time, which Noah Claypole, being hungry and vicious, considered he could not possibly devote to a worthier purpose than aggravating and tantalising young Oliver Twist.

Intent upon this innocent amusement, Noah put his feet on the table-cloth, and pulled Oliver's hair, and twitched his ears, and expressed his opinion that he was a "sneak," and furthermore announced his intention of coming to see him hung whenever that desirable event should take place, and entered upon various other topics of petty annoyance, like a malicious and ill-conditioned charity-boy as he was. But, none of these taunts producing the desired effect of making Oliver cry, Noah attempted to be more facetious still, and in this attempt did what many small wits, with far greater reputations than Noah, notwithstanding, do to this day when they want to be funny;—he got rather personal.

"Work'us," said Noah, "how's your mother?"

"She's dead," replied Oliver; "don't you say anything about her to me!"

Oliver's colour rose as he said this; he breathed quickly, and there was a curious working of the mouth and nostrils, which Mr. Claypole thought must be the immediate precursor of a violent fit of crying. Under this impression, he returned to the charge.

"What did she die of, Work'us?" said Noah.

"Of a broken heart, some of our old nurses told me," replied Oliver, more as if he were talking to himself than answering Noah. "I think I know what it must be to die of that!"

"Tol de rol lol lol, right fol lairy, Work'us," said Noah, as a tear rolled down Oliver's cheek. "What's set you a-snivelling now?"

"Not *you*," replied Oliver, hastily brushing the tear away. "Don't think it."

"Oh, not me, eh?" sneered Noah.

"No, not you," replied Oliver, sharply. "There; that's enough. Don't say anything more to me about her; you'd better not!"

"Better not!" exclaimed Noah. "Well! better not! Work'us, don't be impudent. *Your* mother, too! She was a nice 'un, she was. Oh, Lor!" And here Noah nodded his head expressively, and curled up as much of his small red nose as muscular action could collect together for the occasion.

"Yer know, Work'us," continued Noah, emboldened by Oliver's silence, and speaking in a jeering tone of affected pity—of all tones the most annoying—"Yer know, Work'us, it carn't be helped now, and of course yer couldn't help it then, and I'm very sorry for it, and I'm sure we all are, and pity yer very much. But yer must know, Work'us, yer mother was a regular right-down bad 'un."

" What did you say?" inquired Oliver, looking up very quickly.

" A regular right-down bad 'un, Work'us," replied Noah, coolly; " and it's a great deal better, Work'us, that she died when she did, or else she'd have been hard labouring in Bridewell, or transported, or hung, which is more likely than either, isn't it?"

Crimson with fury, Oliver started up, overthrew chair and table, seized Noah by the throat, shook him in the violence of his rage till his teeth chattered in his head, and, collecting his whole force into one heavy blow, felled him to the ground.

A minute ago the boy had looked the quiet, mild, dejected creature that harsh treatment had made him. But his spirit was roused at last; the cruel insult to his dead mother had set his blood on fire. His breast heaved, his attitude was erect, his eye bright and vivid, and his whole person changed, as he stood glaring over the cowardly tormentor who lay crouching at his feet, and defied him with an energy he had never known before.

"He'll murder me!" blubbered Noah. "Charlotte! missis! here's the new boy a-murdering of me! Help! help! Oliver's gone mad! Char—lotte!"

Noah's shouts were responded to by a loud scream from Charlotte, and a louder from Mrs. Sowerberry; the former of whom rushed into the kitchen by a side-door, while the latter paused on the staircase till she was quite certain that it was consistent with the preservation of human life to come further down.

"Oh, you little wretch!" screamed Charlotte, seizing Oliver with her utmost force, which was about equal to that of a moderately strong man in particularly good training,— "Oh, you little un-grate-ful, mur-de-rous, horrid vil-lain!" and between every syllable Charlotte gave Oliver a blow with all her might, and accompanied it with a scream for the benefit of society.

Charlotte's fist was by no means a light one;

but, lest it should not be effectual in calming Oliver's wrath, Mrs. Sowerberry plunged into the kitchen, and assisted to hold him with one hand, while she scratched his face with the other; in this favourable position of affairs Noah rose from the ground, and pummeled him from behind.

This was rather too violent exercise to last long. When they were all three wearied out, and could tear and beat no longer, they dragged Oliver, struggling and shouting, but nothing daunted, into the dust-cellar, and there locked him up; this being done, Mrs. Sowerberry sunk into a chair, and burst into tears.

"Bless her, she's going off!" said Charlotte. "A glass of water, Noah, dear. Make haste."

"Oh! Charlotte," said Mrs. Sowerberry, speaking as well as she could through a deficiency of breath and a sufficiency of cold water which Noah had poured over her head and shoulders,—"Oh! Charlotte, what a mercy we have not been all murdered in our beds!"

"Ah! mercy indeed, ma'am," was the reply. "I only hope this 'll teach master not to have any more of these dreadful creatures that are born to be murderers and robbers from their very cradle. Poor Noah! he was all but killed, ma'am, when I came in."

" Poor fellow!" said Mrs. Sowerberry, looking piteously on the charity-boy.

Noah, whose top waistcoat-button might have been somewhere on a level with the crown of Oliver's head, rubbed his eyes with the inside of his wrists while this commiseration was bestowed upon him, and performed some affecting tears and sniffs.

" What's to be done!" exclaimed Mrs. Sowerberry. " Your master's not at home,—there's not a man in the house,—and he'll kick that door down in ten minutes." Oliver's vigorous plunges against the bit of timber in question rendered this occurrence highly probable.

" Dear, dear! I don't know, ma'am," said Charlotte, " unless we send for the police-officers."

" Or the millingtary," suggested Mr. Claypole.

" No, no," said Mrs. Sowerberry, bethinking herself of Oliver's old friend; " run to Mr. Bumble, Noah, and tell him to come here directly, and not to lose a minute; never mind your cap—make haste. You can hold a knife to that black eye as you run along, and it'll keep the swelling down."

Noah stopped to make no reply, but started off at his fullest speed; and very much it astonished the people who were out walking, to see a charity-boy tearing through the streets pellmell, with no cap on his head, and a clasp-knife at his eye.

CHAPTER VII.

OLIVER CONTINUES REFRACTORY.

Noah Claypole ran along the streets at his swiftest pace, and paused not once for breath until he reached the workhouse-gate. Having rested here for a minute or so, to collect a good burst of sobs and an imposing show of tears and terror, he knocked loudly at the wicket, and presented such a rueful face to the aged pauper who opened it, that even he, who saw nothing but rueful faces about him at the best of times, started back in astonishment.

"Why, what's the matter with the boy?" said the old pauper.

"Mr. Bumble! Mr. Bumble!" cried Noah, with well-affected dismay, and in tones so loud and agitated that they not only caught the ear of Mr. Bumble himself, who happened to be hard by, but alarmed him so much that he rushed into the yard without his cocked hat,— which is a very curious and remarkable circumstance, as showing that even a beadle, acted upon by a sudden and powerful impulse, may be afflicted with a momentary visitation of loss of self-possession, and forgetfulness of personal dignity.

"Oh, Mr. Bumble, sir!" said Noah: "Oliver, sir,—Oliver has ——"

"What?—what?" interposed Mr. Bumble, with a gleam of pleasure in his metallic eyes. "Not run away; he hasn't run away, has he, Noah?"

"No, sir, no; not run away, sir, but he's turned wicious," replied Noah. "He tried to murder me, sir, and then he tried to murder Charlotte, and then missis. Oh! what dreadful pain it is! such agony, please, sir!" and here Noah writhed and twisted his body into an extensive variety of eel-like positions; thereby giving Mr. Bumble to understand that, from the violent and sanguinary onset of Oliver

Twist, he had sustained severe internal injury and damage, from which he was at that moment suffering the acutest torture.

When Noah saw that the intelligence he communicated perfectly paralyzed Mr. Bumble, he imparted additional effect thereunto, by bewailing his dreadful wounds ten times louder than before; and, when he observed a gentleman in a white waistcoat crossing the yard, he was more tragic in his lamentations than ever, rightly conceiving it highly expedient to attract the notice, and rouse the indignation, of the gentleman aforesaid.

The gentleman's notice was very soon attracted, for he had not walked three paces when he turned angrily round, and inquired what that young cur was howling for, and why Mr. Bumble did not favour him with something which would render the series of vocular exclamations so designated, an involuntary process.

"It's a poor boy from the free-school, sir," replied Mr. Bumble, "who has been nearly murdered—all but murdered, sir—by young Twist."

"By Jove!" exclaimed the gentleman in the white waistcoat, stopping short. "I knew it! I felt a strange presentiment from the very first, that that audacious young savage would come to be hung!"

"He has likewise attempted, sir, to murder the female servant," said Mr. Bumble, with a face of ashy paleness.

"And his missis," interposed Mr. Claypole.

"And his master, too, I think you said, Noah?" added Mr. Bumble.

"No; he's out, or he would have murdered him," replied Noah. "He said he wanted to—"

"Ah! said he wanted to—did he, my boy?" inquired the gentleman in the white waistcoat.

"Yes, sir," replied Noah; "and please, sir, missis wants to know whether Mr. Bumble can spare time to step up there directly and flog him, 'cause master's out."

"Certainly, my boy; certainly," said the gentleman in the white waistcoat, smiling benignly, and patting Noah's head, which was about three inches higher than his own.

"You're a good boy—a very good boy. Here's a penny for you. Bumble, just step up to Sowerberry's with your cane, and see what's best to be done. Don't spare him, Bumble."

"No, I will not sir," replied the beadle, adjusting the wax-end which was twisted round the bottom of his cane for purposes of parochial flagellation.

"Tell Sowerberry not to spare him either. They'll never do anything with him without stripes and bruises," said the gentleman in the white waistcoat.

"I'll take care, sir," replied the beadle. And the cocked hat and cane having been by this time adjusted to their owner's satisfaction, Mr. Bumble and Noah Claypole betook themselves with all speed to the undertaker's shop.

Here the position of affairs had not at all improved, or Sowerberry had not yet returned, and Oliver continued to kick with undiminished vigour at the cellar-door. The accounts of his ferocity, as related by Mrs. Sowerberry and

Charlotte, were of so startling a nature that Mr. Bumble judged it prudent to parley before opening the door. With this view he gave a kick at the outside, by way of prelude, and then, applying his mouth to the keyhole, said, in a deep and impressive tone,

"Oliver!"

"Come; you let me out!" replied Oliver, from the inside.

"Do you know this here voice, Oliver?" said Mr. Bumble.

"Yes," replied Oliver.

"Ain't you afraid of it, sir? Ain't you a-tremling while I speak, sir?" said Mr. Bumble.

"No!" replied Oliver boldly.

An answer so different from the one he had expected to elicit, and was in the habit of receiving, staggered Mr. Bumble not a little. He stepped back from the keyhole, drew himself up to his full height, and looked from one to another of the three by-standers in mute astonishment.

"Oh, you know Mr. Bumble, he must

be mad," said Mrs. Sowerberry. "No boy in half his senses could venture to speak so to you."

"It's not madness, ma'am," replied Mr. Bumble, after a few moments of deep meditation; "it's meat."

"What!" exclaimed Mrs. Sowerberry.

"Meat, ma'am, meat," replied Bumble, with stern emphasis. "You've overfed him, ma'am. You've raised a artificial soul and spirit in him, ma'am, unbecoming a person of his condition, as the board, Mrs. Sowerberry, who are practical philosophers, will tell you. What have paupers to do with soul or spirit either? It's quite enough that we let 'em have live bodies. If you had kept the boy on gruel, ma'am, this would never have happened."

"Dear, dear!" ejaculated Mrs. Sowerberry, piously raising her eyes to the kitchen ceiling, "this comes of being liberal!"

The liberality of Mrs. Sowerberry to Oliver had consisted in a profuse bestowal upon him of all the dirty odds and ends which nobody else would eat; so that there was a great deal of meekness and self-devotion in her voluntarily remaining under Mr. Bumble's heavy accusation, of which, to do her justice, she was wholly innocent in thought, word, or deed.

"Ah!" said Mr. Bumble, when the lady brought her eyes down to earth again; "the only thing that can be done now, that I know of, is to leave him in the cellar for a day or so till he's a little starved down, and then to take him out and keep him on gruel all through his apprenticeship. He comes of a bad family—excitable natures, Mrs. Sowerberry. Both the nurse and doctor said that that mother of his made her way here against difficulties and pain that would have killed any well-disposed woman weeks before."

At this point of Mr. Bumble's discourse, Oliver just hearing enough to know that some further allusion was being made to his mother, recommenced kicking with a violence which rendered every other sound inaudible. Sowerberry returned at this juncture, and Oliver's offence having been explained to him, with such exaggerations as the ladies thought best calculated to rouse his ire, he unlocked the cellar-door in a twinkling, and dragged his rebellious apprentice out by the collar.

Oliver's clothes had been torn in the beating he had received; his face was bruised and scratched, and his hair scattered over his forehead. The angry flush had not disappeared, however; and when he was pulled out of his prison, he scowled boldly on Noah, and looked quite undismayed.

"Now, you are a nice young fellow, ain't you?" said Sowerberry, giving Oliver a shake and a box on the ear.

"He called my mother names," replied Oliver.

"Well, and what if he did, you little ungrateful wretch?" said Mrs. Sowerberry. "She deserved what he said, and worse."

"She didn't," said Oliver.

"She did," said Mrs. Sowerberry.

"It's a lie!" said Oliver.

Mrs. Sowerberry burst into a flood of tears.

This flood of tears left Sowerberry no alternative. If he had hesitated for one instant to punish Oliver most severely, it must be quite clear to every experienced reader that he would have been, according to all precedents in disputes of matrimony established, a brute, an unnatural husband, an insulting creature, a base imitation of a man, and various other agreeable characters too numerous for recital within the limits of this chapter. To do him justice, he was, as far as his power went,—it was not very extensive, —kindly disposed towards the boy; perhaps because it was his interest to be so, perhaps because his wife disliked him. The flood of tears, however, left him no resource; so he at once gave him a drubbing, which satisfied even Mrs. Sowerberry herself, and rendered Mr. Bumble's subsequent application of the parochial cane rather unnecessary. For the rest of the day he was shut up in the back kitchen, in company with a pump and a slice of bread; and, at night, Mrs. Sowerberry, after making various remarks outside the door, by no means complimentary to the memory of his mother, looked into the room, and, amidst the jeers and pointings of Noah and Charlotte, ordered him up stairs to his dismal bed.

It was not until he was left alone in the silence and stillness of the gloomy workshop of the undertaker, that Oliver gave way to the feelings which the day's treatment may be supposed likely to have awakened in a mere child. He had listened to their taunts with a look of contempt; he had borne the lash without a cry, for he felt that pride swelling in his heart which would have kept down a shriek to the last, if they had roasted him alive. But, now, that there were none to see or hear him, he fell upon his knees on the floor, and, hiding his face in his hands, wept such tears as, God send for the credit of our nature, few so young may ever have cause to pour out before him.

For a long time Oliver remained motionless in this attitude. The candle was burning low in the socket when he rose to his feet, and having gazed cautiously round him, and listened intently, gently undid the fastenings of the door and looked abroad.

It was a cold dark night. The stars seemed to the boy's eyes further from the earth than he had ever seen them before; there was no wind;

and the sombre shadows thrown by the trees on the earth, looked sepulchral and death-like, from being so still. He softly reclosed the door, and, having availed himself of the expiring light of the candle to tie up in a handkerchief the few articles of wearing apparel he had, sat himself down upon a bench to wait for morning.

With the first ray of light that struggled through the crevices in the shutters Oliver rose, and again unbarred the door. One timid look around,—one moment's pause of hesitation,— he had closed it behind him, and was in the open street.

He looked to the right and to the left, uncertain whither to fly. He remembered to have seen the waggons, as they went out, toiling up the hill; he took the same route, and arriving at a footpath across the fields, which he knew after some distance led out again into the road, struck into it, and walked quickly on.

Along this same footpath Oliver well remembered he had trotted beside Mr. Bumble, when he first carried him to the workhouse from the farm. His way lay directly in front of the cottage. His heart beat quickly when he bethought himself of this, and he half resolved to turn back. He had come a long way though, and should lose a great deal of time by doing so. Besides, it was so early that there was very little fear of his being seen; so he walked on.

He reached the house. There was no appearance of its inmates stirring at that early hour. Oliver stopped, and peeped into the garden. A child was weeding one of the little beds; and as he stopped, he raised his pale face, and disclosed the features of one of his former companions. Oliver felt glad to see him before he went, for, though younger than himself, he had been his little friend and playmate; they had been beaten, and starved, and shut up together, many and many a time.

" Hush, Dick!" said Oliver, as the boy ran to the gate, and thrust his thin arm between the rails to greet him. " Is any one up?"

" Nobody but me," replied the child.

" You mustn't say you saw me, Dick," said Oliver; " I am running away. They beat and ill-use me, Dick; and I am going to seek my fortune, some long way off, I don't know where. How pale you are!"

"I heard the doctor tell them I was dying," replied the child with a faint smile. "I am very glad to see you, dear; but don't stop, don't stop."

"Yes, yes, I will, to say good-b'ye to you," replied Oliver. "I shall see you again, Dick; I know I shall. You will be well and happy."

"I hope so," replied the child, "after I am dead, but not before. I know the doctor must be right, Oliver, because I dream so much of heaven and angels, and kind faces that I never see when I am awake. "Kiss me," said the child, climbing up the low gate, and flinging his little arms round Oliver's neck. "Good-b'ye, dear! God bless you!"

The blessing was from a young child's lips, but it was the first that Oliver had ever heard invoked upon his head; and through all the struggles and sufferings, and troubles and changes of his after life, he never once forgot it.

CHAPTER VIII.

OLIVER WALKS TO LONDON, AND ENCOUNTERS ON THE ROAD A STRANGE SORT OF YOUNG GENTLEMAN.

OLIVER reached the style at which the bypath terminated, and once more gained the high-road. It was eight o'clock now; and, though he was nearly five miles away from the town, he ran, and hid behind the hedges by turns, till noon, fearing that he might be pursued and overtaken. Then he sat down to rest by the side of a mile-stone, and began to think for the first time where he had better go and try to live.

The stone by which he was seated bore in large characters an intimation that it was just seventy miles from that spot to London. The name awakened a new train of ideas in the boy's mind. London!—that great large place!

—nobody—not even Mr. Bumble—could ever find him there. He had often heard the old men in the workhouse, too, say that no lad of spirit need want in London, and that there were ways of living in that vast city which those who had been bred up in country parts had no idea of. It was the very place for a homeless boy, who must die in the streets unless some one helped him. As these things passed through his thoughts, he jumped upon his feet, and again walked forward.

He had diminished the distance between himself and London by full four miles more, before he recollected how much he must undergo ere he could hope to reach his place of destination. As this consideration forced itself upon him, he slackened his pace a little, and meditated upon his means of getting there. He had a crust of bread, a coarse shirt, and two pairs of stockings in his bundle; and a penny—a gift of Sowerberry's after some funeral in which he had acquitted himself more than ordinarily well—in his pocket. "A clean shirt," thought Oliver, "is a very comfortable thing,—very; and so are two pairs of darned stockings, and so is a penny, but they are small helps to a sixty-five miles' walk in winter time." But Oliver's thoughts, like those of most other people, although they were extremely ready and active to point out his difficulties, were wholly at a loss to suggest any feasible mode of surmounting them; so, after a good deal of thinking to no particular purpose, he changed his little bundle over to the other shoulder, and trudged on.

Oliver walked twenty miles that day, and all that time tasted nothing but the crust of dry bread, and a few draughts of water which he begged at the cottage-doors by the road-side. When the night came, he turned into a meadow, and, creeping close under a hay-rick, determined to lie there till morning. He felt frightened at first, for the wind moaned dismally over the empty fields, and he was cold and hungry, and more alone than he had ever felt before. Being very tired with his walk, however, he soon fell asleep and forgot his troubles.

He felt cold and stiff when he got up next

morning, and so hungry that he was obliged to exchange the penny for a small loaf in the very first village through which he passed. He had walked no more than twelve miles, when night closed in again; for his feet were sore, and his legs so weak that they trembled beneath him. Another night passed in the bleak damp air only made him worse; and, when he set forward on his journey next morning, he could hardly crawl along.

He waited at the bottom of a steep hill till a stage-coach came up, and then begged of the outside passengers; but there were very few who took any notice of him, and even those, told him to wait till they got to the top of the hill, and then let them see how far he could run for a halfpenny. Poor Oliver tried to keep up with the coach a little way, but was unable to do it, by reason of his fatigue and sore feet. When the outsides saw this, they put their halfpence back into their pockets again, declaring that he was an idle young dog, and didn't deserve anything; and the coach rattled away, and left only a cloud of dust behind.

In some villages large painted boards were fixed up warning all persons who begged within the district that they would be sent to jail, which frightened Oliver very much, and made him very glad to get out of them with all possible expedition. In others he would stand about the inn-yards, and look mournfully at every one who passed; a proceeding which generally terminated in the landlady's ordering one of the post-boys who were lounging about, to drive that strange boy out of the place, for she was sure he had come to steal something. If he begged at a farmer's house, ten to one but they threatened to set the dog on him; and when he showed his nose in a shop, they talked about the beadle, which brought Oliver's heart into his mouth,—very often the only thing he had there, for many hours together.

In fact, if it had not been for a good-hearted turnpike-man, and a benevolent old lady, Oliver's troubles would have been shortened by the very same process which put an end to his mother's; in other words, he would most assuredly have fallen dead upon the king's highway. But the turnpike-man gave him a meal of bread and cheese; and the old lady, who had a shipwrecked grandson wandering barefooted in some distant part of the earth, took pity upon the poor orphan, and gave him what little she could afford—and more—with such kind and gentle words, and such tears of sympathy and compassion, that they sank deeper into Oliver's soul than all the sufferings he had ever undergone.

Early on the seventh morning after he had left his native place, Oliver limped slowly into the little town of Barnet. The window shutters were closed, the street was empty, not a soul had awakened to the business of the day. The sun was rising in all his splendid beauty, but the light only served to show the boy his own lonesomeness and desolation as he sat with bleeding feet and covered with dust upon a cold door-step.

By degrees the shutters were opened, the window-blinds were drawn up, and people began passing to and fro. Some few stopped to gaze at Oliver for a moment or two, or turned round to stare at him as they hurried by; but none relieved him, or troubled themselves to inquire how he came there. He had no heart to beg, and there he sat.

He had been crouching on the step for some time, wondering at the great number of public houses (every other house in Barnet is a tavern, large or small), gazing listlessly at the coaches as they passed through, and thinking how strange it seemed that they could do with ease in a few hours what it had taken him a whole week of courage and determination beyond his years to accomplish, when he was roused by observing that a boy who had passed him carelessly some minutes before, had returned, and was now surveying him most earnestly from the opposite side of the way. He took little heed of this at first; but the boy remained in the same attitude of close observation so long, that Oliver raised his head, and returned his steady look. Upon this, the boy crossed over, and, walking close up to Oliver, said,

"Hullo! my covey, what's the row?"

The boy who addressed this inquiry to the young wayfarer was about his own age, but one of the queerest-looking boys that Oliver had ever seen. He was a snub-nosed, flat-browed, common-faced boy enough, and as dirty a juvenile as one would wish to see; but he had about him all the airs and manners of a man. He was short of his age, with rather bow-legs, and little sharp ugly eyes. His hat was stuck on the top of his head so slightly that it threatened to fall off every moment, and would have done so very often if the wearer had not had a knack of every now and then giving his head a sudden twitch, which brought it back to its old place again. He wore a man's coat, which reached nearly to his heels. He had turned the cuffs back halfway up his arm to get his hands out of the sleeves, apparently with the ultimate view of thrusting them into the pockets of his corduroy trousers, for there he kept them. He was altogether as roystering and swaggering a young gentleman as ever stood four feet six, or something less, in his bluchers.

"Hullo, my covey, what's the row?" said this strange young gentleman to Oliver.

"I am very hungry and tired," replied Oliver, the tears standing in his eyes as he spoke. "I have walked a long way—I have been walking these seven days."

"Walking for sivin days!" said the young gentleman. "Oh, I see. Beak's order, eh? But," he added, noticing Oliver's look of surprise, "I suppose you don't know what a beak is, my flash com-pan-i-on."

Oliver mildly replied, that he had always heard a bird's mouth described by the term in question.

"My eyes, how green!" exclaimed the young gentleman. "Why, a beak's a madgst'rate; and when you walk by a beak's order, it's not straight forerd, but always going up, and nivir coming down agen. Was you never on the mill?"

"What mill?" inquired Oliver.

"What mill!—why, *the* mill—the mill as takes up so little room that'll work inside a stone jug, and always goes better when the wind's low with people than when it's high, acos then they can't get workmen. But come," said the young gentleman; "you want grub, and you shall have it. I'm at low-water-mark—only one bob and a magpie; but, *as* far *as* it goes, I'll fork out and stump. Up with you on your pins. There: now then. Morrice."

Assisting Oliver to rise, the young gentleman took him to an adjacent chandler's shop, where he purchased a sufficiency of ready-dressed ham and a half-quartern loaf, or, as he himself expressed it, "a fourpenny bran;" the ham being kept clean and preserved from dust by the ingenious expedient of making a hole in the loaf by pulling out a portion of the crumb, and stuffing it therein. Taking the bread under his arm, the young gentleman turned into a small public-house, and led the way to a tap-room in the rear of the premises. Here, a pot of beer was brought in by the direction of the mysterious youth; and Oliver, falling to, at his new friend's bidding, made a long and hearty meal, during the progress of which the strange boy eyed him from time to time with great attention.

"Going to London?" said the strange boy, when Oliver had at length concluded.

"Yes."

"Got any lodgings?"

"No."

"Money?"

"No."

The strange boy whistled, and put his arms into his pockets as far as the big-coat sleeves would let them go.

"Do you live in London?" inquired Oliver.

"Yes, I do, when I'm at home," replied the boy. "I suppose you want some place to sleep in to-night, don't you?"

"I do indeed," answered Oliver. "I have not slept under a roof since I left the country."

"Don't fret your eyelids on that score," said the young gentleman. "I've got to be in London to-night, and I know a 'spectable old genelman as lives there, wot'll give you lodgings for nothink, and never ask for the change; that is, if any genelman he knows interduces you. And don't he know me?—Oh, no—not in the least—by no means—certainly not."

The young gentleman smiled, as if to intimate that the latter fragments of discourse were playfully ironical, and finished the beer as he did so.

This unexpected offer of shelter was too tempting to be resisted, especially as it was immediately followed up by the assurance that the old gentleman already referred to, would doubtless provide Oliver with a comfortable place without loss of time. This led to a more friendly and confidential dialogue, from which Oliver discovered that his friend's name was Jack Dawkins, and that he was a peculiar pet and *protegé* of the elderly gentleman before mentioned.

Mr. Dawkins's appearance did not say a vast deal in favour of the comforts which his patron's interest obtained for those whom he took under his protection; but as he had a rather flighty and dissolute mode of conversing, and furthermore avowed that among his intimate friends he was better known by the *soubriquet* of " The artful Dodger," Oliver concluded that, being of a dissipated and careless turn, the moral precepts of his benefactor had hitherto been thrown away upon him. Under this impression, he secretly resolved to cultivate the good opinion of the old gentleman as quickly as possible; and, if he found the Dodger incorrigible, as he more than half suspected he should, to decline the honour of his farther acquaintance.

As John Dawkins objected to their entering London before nightfall, it was nearly eleven o'clock when they reached the turnpike at Islington. They crossed from the Angel into St. John's-road, struck down the small street which terminates at Sadler's Wells theatre, through Exmouth-street and Coppice-row, down the little court by the side of the workhouse, across the classic ground which once bore the name of Hockley-in-the-Hole, thence into Little Saffron-hill, and so into Saffron-hill the Great, along which the Dodger scudded at a rapid pace, directing Oliver to follow close at his heels.

Although Oliver had enough to occupy his attention in keeping sight of his leader, he could not help bestowing a few hasty glances on either side of the way as he passed along. A dirtier or more wretched place he had never seen. The street was very narrow and muddy, and the air was impregnated with filthy odours. There were a good many small shops; but the only stock in trade appeared to be heaps of children, who, even at that time of night, were crawling in and out at the doors, or screaming from the inside. The sole places that seemed to prosper amid the general blight of the place were the public-houses, and in them, the lowest orders of Irish (who are generally the lowest orders of anything) were wrangling with might and main. Covered ways and yards, which here and there diverged from the main street, disclosed little knots of houses where drunken men and women were positively wallowing in the filth; and from several of the door-ways, great ill-looking fellows were cautiously emerging, bound, to all appearance, upon no very well-disposed or harmless errands.

Oliver was just considering whether he

hadn't better run away, when they reached the bottom of the hill: his conductor catching him by the arm, pushed open the door of a house near Field-lane, and, drawing him into the passage, closed it behind them.

"Now, then," cried a voice from below, in reply to a whistle from the Dodger.

"*Plummy and slam!*" was the reply.

This seemed to be some watchword or signal that all was right; for the light of a feeble candle gleamed on the wall at the farther end of the passage, and a man's face peeped out from where a balustrade of the old kitchen staircase had been broken away.

"There's two on you," said the man, thrusting the candle farther out, and shading his eyes with his hand. "Who's the t'other one?"

"A new pal," replied Jack Dawkins, pulling Oliver forward.

"Where did he come from?"

"Greenland. Is Fagin up stairs?"

"Yes, he's a sortin' the wipes. Up with you." The candle was drawn back, and the face disappeared.

Oliver, groping his way with one hand, and with the other firmly grasped by his companion, ascended with much difficulty the dark and broken stairs, which his conductor mounted with an ease and expedition that showed he was well acquainted with them. He threw open the door of a back-room, and drew Oliver in after him.

The walls and ceiling of the room were perfectly black with age and dirt. There was a deal table before the fire, upon which was a candle stuck in a ginger-beer bottle; two or three pewter pots, a loaf and butter, and a plate. In a frying-pan which was on the fire, and which was secured to the mantelshelf by a string, some sausages were cooking; and standing over them, with a toasting-fork in his hand, was a very old shrivelled Jew, whose villanous-looking and repulsive face was obscured by a quantity of matted red hair. He was dressed in a greasy flannel gown, with his throat bare, and seemed to be dividing his attention between the frying-pan and a clothes-horse, over which a great number of silk handkerchiefs were hanging. Several rough beds made of old sacks were huddled side by side on the floor; and seated round the table were four or five boys, none older than the Dodger, smoking long clay pipes and drinking spirits with the air of middle-aged men. These all crowded about their associate as he whispered a few words to the Jew, and then turned round and grinned at Oliver, as did the Jew himself: toasting-fork in hand.

" This is him, Fagin," said Jack Dawkins; " my friend, Oliver Twist."

The Jew grinned; and, making a low obeisance to Oliver, took him by the hand, and hoped he should have the honour of his intimate acquaintance. Upon this, the young gentlemen with the pipes came round him, and shook both his hands very hard — especially the one in which he held his little bundle. One young gentleman was very anxious to hang up his cap for him; and another was so obliging as to put his hands in his pockets, in order that, as he was very tired, he might not have the trouble of emptying them when he went to

George Cruikshank

bed. These civilities would probably have been extended much further, but for a liberal exercise of the Jew's toasting-fork on the heads and shoulders of the affectionate youths who offered them.

"We are very glad to see you, Oliver—very," said the Jew. "Dodger, take off the sausages, and draw a tub near the fire for Oliver. Ah, you're a-staring at the pocket-handkerchiefs! eh, my dear? There are a good many of 'em, ain't there? We've just looked 'em out ready for the wash; that's all, Oliver; that's all. Ha! ha! ha!"

The latter part of this speech was hailed by a boisterous shout from all the hopeful pupils of the merry old gentleman, in the midst of which they went to supper.

Oliver ate his share; and the Jew then mixed him a glass of hot gin and water, telling him he must drink it off directly, because another gentleman wanted the tumbler. Oliver did as he was desired. Almost instantly afterwards, he felt himself gently lifted on to one of the sacks, and then he sunk into a deep sleep.

CHAPTER IX.

CONTAINING FURTHER PARTICULARS CONCERNING THE PLEASANT OLD GENTLEMAN, AND HIS HOPEFUL PUPILS.

It was late next morning when Oliver awoke from a sound, long sleep. There was no other person in the room but the old Jew, who was boiling some coffee in a saucepan for breakfast, and whistling softly to himself as he stirred it round and round with an iron spoon. He would stop every now and then to listen when there was the least noise below; and, when he had satisfied himself, he would go on whistling and stirring again as before.

Although Oliver had roused himself from sleep, he was not thoroughly awake. There is a drowsy state, between sleeping and waking, when you dream more in five minutes with your eyes half open, and yourself half conscious of everything that is passing around you, than you would in five nights with your eyes fast closed, and your senses wrapt in perfect unconsciousness. At such times, a mortal knows just enough of what his mind is doing to form some glimmering conception of its mighty powers, its bounding from earth and spurning time and space, when freed from the restraint of its corporeal associate.

Oliver was precisely in this condition. He saw the Jew with his half-closed eyes, heard his low whistling, and recognised the sound of the spoon grating against the saucepan's sides; and yet the self-same senses were mentally engaged at the same time in busy action with almost everybody he had ever known.

When the coffee was done, the Jew drew the saucepan to the hob, and, standing in an irresolute attitude for a few minutes, as if he did not well know how to employ himself, turned round and looked at Oliver, and called him by his name. He did not answer, and was to all appearance asleep.

After satisfying himself upon this head, the Jew stepped gently to the door, which he fastened; he then drew forth, as it seemed to Oliver, from some trap in the floor, a small box, which he placed carefully on the table. His eyes glistened as he raised the lid and looked in. Dragging an old chair to the table, he sat down, and took from it a magnificent gold watch, sparkling with diamonds.

"Aha!" said the Jew, shrugging up his shoulders, and distorting every feature with a hideous grin. "Clever dogs! clever dogs!—Staunch to the last! Never told the old parson where they were; never peached upon old Fagin. And why should they? It wouldn't have loosened the knot, or kept the drop up a minute longer. No, no, no! Fine fellows!—fine fellows!"

With these and other muttered reflections of the like nature, the Jew once more deposited the watch in its place of safety. At least half a dozen more were severally drawn forth from the same box, and surveyed with equal pleasure; besides rings, brooches, bracelets, and other articles of jewellery, of such magnificent materials and costly workmanship that Oliver had no idea even of their names.

Having replaced these trinkets, the Jew took out another, so small that it lay in the palm of his hand. There seemed to be some very minute inscription on it, for the Jew laid it flat upon the table, and, shading it with his hand, pored over it long and earnestly. At length he put it down as if despairing of success, and, leaning back in his chair, muttered—

" What a fine thing capital punishment is! Dead men never repent; dead men never bring awkward stories to light. Ah, it's a fine thing for the trade! Five of them sprung up in a row, and none left to play booty or turn white-livered!"

As the Jew uttered these words, his bright dark eyes which had been staring vacantly before him, fell on Oliver's face; the boy's eyes were fixed on his in mute curiosity, and, although the recognition was only for an instant—for the briefest space of time that can possibly be conceived—it was enough to show the old man that he had been observed. He closed the lid of the box with a loud crash, and, laying his hand on a bread-knife which was on the table, started furiously up. He trembled very much though; for, even in his terror, Oliver could see that the knife quivered in the air.

"What's that?" said the Jew. "What do you watch me for? Why are you awake? What have you seen? Speak out, boy! Quick—quick! for your life!"

"I wasn't able to sleep any longer, sir," replied Oliver, meekly. "I am very sorry if I have disturbed you, sir."

"You were not awake an hour ago?" said the Jew, scowling fiercely on the boy.

"No—no, indeed, sir," replied Oliver.

"Are you sure?" cried the Jew, with a still fiercer look than before, and a threatening attitude.

"Upon my word I was not, sir," replied Oliver, earnestly. "I was not, indeed, sir."

"Tush, tush, my dear!" said the Jew, abruptly resuming his old manner, and playing with the knife a little, before he laid it down, as if to induce the belief that he had caught it up in mere sport. " Of course I know that, my dear. I only tried to frighten you. You're a brave boy. Ha! ha! you're a brave boy, Oliver!" and the Jew rubbed his hands with a chuckle, but looked uneasily at the box notwithstanding.

" Did you see any of these pretty things, my dear?" said the Jew, laying his hand upon it after a short pause.

" Yes, sir," replied Oliver.

" Ah!" said the Jew, turning rather pale. " They—they're mine, Oliver; my little property. All I have to live upon in my old age. The folks call me a miser, my dear—only a miser; that's all."

Oliver thought the old gentleman must be a decided miser to live in such a dirty place, with so many watches; but, thinking that perhaps his fondness for the Dodger and the other boys cost him a good deal of money, he only cast a deferential look at the Jew, and asked if he might get up.

"Certainly, my dear—certainly," replied the old gentleman. " Stay. There's a pitcher of water in the corner by the door. Bring it here, and I'll give you a basin to wash in, my dear."

Oliver got up, walked across the room, and stooped for one instant to raise the pitcher. When he turned his head, the box was gone.

He had scarcely washed himself and made everything tidy by emptying the basin out of the window, agreeably to the Jew's directions, than the Dodger returned, accompanied by a very sprightly young friend whom Oliver had seen smoking on the previous night, and who was now formally introduced to him as Charley Bates. The four sat down to breakfast upon the coffee and some hot rolls and ham which the Dodger had brought home in the crown of his hat.

" Well," said the Jew, glancing slyly at Oliver, and addressing himself to the Dodger, " I hope you've been at work this morning, my dears."

" Hard," replied the Dodger.

" As nails," added Charley Bates.

" Good boys, good boys!" said the Jew. " What have *you* got, Dodger!"

" A couple of pocket-books," replied that young gentleman.

" Lined?" inquired the Jew with trembling eagerness.

" Pretty well," replied the Dodger, producing two pocket-books, one green and the other red.

" Not so heavy as they might be," said the Jew, after looking at the insides carefully; " but very neat and nicely made. Ingenious workman, ain't he, Oliver?"

" Very, indeed, sir," said Oliver. At which Mr. Charles Bates laughed uproariously, very much to the amazement of Oliver, who saw nothing to laugh at, in anything that had passed.

" And what have you got, my dear?" said Fagin to Charley Bates.

" Wipes," replied Master Bates: at the same time producing four pocket-handkerchiefs.

" Well," said the Jew, inspecting them

closely; " They're very good ones—very. You haven't marked them well, though, Charley; so the marks shall be picked out with a needle, and we'll teach Oliver how to do it. Shall us, Oliver, eh?—Ha! ha! ha!"

" If you please, sir," said Oliver.

" You'd like to be able to make pocket-handkerchiefs as easy as Charley Bates, wouldn't you, my dear?" said the Jew.

" Very much indeed, if you'll teach me, sir," replied Oliver.

Master Bates saw something so exquisitely ludicrous in this reply that he burst into another laugh; which laugh meeting the coffee he was drinking, and carrying it down some wrong channel, very nearly terminated in his premature suffocation.

" He is so jolly green!" said Charley when he recovered, as an apology to the company for his unpolite behaviour.

The Dodger said nothing, but he smoothed Oliver's hair down over his eyes, and said he'd know better by-and-by; upon which the old gentleman, observing Oliver's colour mounting, changed the subject by asking whether there had been much of a crowd at the execution that morning. This made him wonder more and more, for it was plain from the replies of the two boys that they had both been there, and Oliver naturally wondered how they could possibly have found time to be so very industrious.

When the breakfast was cleared away, the merry old gentleman and the two boys played at a very curious and uncommon game, which was performed in this way:—The merry old gentleman, placing a snuff-box in one pocket of his trousers, a note-case in the other, and a watch in his waistcoat pocket, with a guard chain round his neck,—and sticking a mock diamond pin in his shirt, buttoned his coat tight round him, and, putting his spectacle-case and handkerchief in the pockets, trotted up and down the room with a stick, in imitation of the manner in which old gentlemen walk about the streets every hour in the day. Sometimes he stopped at the fire-place, and sometimes at the door, making belief that he was staring with all his might into shop-windows. At such times he would look constantly round him for fear of thieves, and keep slapping all his pockets in turn, to see that he hadn't lost anything, in such a very funny and natural manner, that Oliver laughed till the tears ran down his face. All this time the two boys followed him closely about, getting out of his sight so nimbly every time he turned round, that it was impossible to follow their motions. At last the Dodger trod upon his toes, or ran upon his boot accidentally, while Charley Bates stumbled up against him behind; and in that one moment they took from him with the most extraordinary rapidity snuff-box, note case, watch-guard, chain, shirt-pin, pocket-handkerchief,—even the spectacle-case. If the old gentleman felt a hand in any one of his pockets, he cried out where it was, and then the game began all over again.

When this game had been played a great many times, a couple of young ladies came to see the young gentlemen; one of whom was called Bet, and the other Nancy. They wore a good deal of hair, not very neatly turned up behind, and were rather untidy about the shoes and stockings. They were not exactly pretty, perhaps; but they had a great deal of colour in their faces, and looked quite stout and hearty. Being remarkably free and agreeable in their manners, Oliver thought them very nice girls indeed, as there is no doubt they were.

These visitors stopped a long time. Spirits were produced, in consequence of one of the young ladies complaining of a coldness in her inside, and the conversation took a very convivial and improving turn. At length Charley Bates expressed his opinion that it was time to pad the hoof, which it occurred to Oliver must be French for going out; for directly afterwards, the Dodger, and Charley, and the two young ladies, went away together, having been kindly furnished with money to spend by the amiable old Jew.

"There, my dear," said Fagin, "that's a pleasant life, isn't it? They have gone out for the day."

"Have they done work, sir?" inquired Oliver.

"Yes," said the Jew; "that is, unless they should unexpectedly come across any when they are out; and they won't neglect it if they do, my dear, depend upon it."

"Make 'em your models, my dear, make 'em your models," said the Jew, tapping the fire-shovel on the hearth to add force to his words; "do everything they bid you, and take their advice in all matters, especially the Dodger's, my dear. He'll be a great man himself, and make you one too, if you take pattern by him. Is my handkerchief hanging out of my pocket, my dear?" said the Jew, stopping short.

"Yes, sir," said Oliver.

"See if you can take it out without my feeling it, as you saw them do, when we were at play this morning."

Oliver held up the bottom of the pocket with one hand as he had seen the Dodger hold it, and drew the handkerchief lightly out of it with the other.

"Is it gone?" cried the Jew.

"Here it is, sir," said Oliver, showing it in his hand.

"You're a clever boy, my dear," said the playful old gentleman, patting Oliver on the head approvingly; "I never saw a sharper lad. Here's a shilling for you. If you go on in this way, you'll be the greatest man of the time. And now come here, and I'll show you how to take the marks out of the handkerchiefs."

Oliver wondered what picking the old gentleman's pocket in play had to do with his chances of being a great man; but thinking that the Jew, being so much his senior, must know best, followed him quietly to the table, and was soon deeply involved in his new study.

CHAPTER X.

OLIVER BECOMES BETTER ACQUAINTED WITH THE CHARACTERS OF HIS NEW ASSOCIATES, AND PURCHASES EXPERIENCE AT A HIGH PRICE. BEING A SHORT BUT VERY IMPORTANT CHAPTER IN THIS HISTORY.

For many days Oliver remained in the Jew's room, picking the marks out of the pocket-handkerchiefs, (of which a great number were brought home,) and sometimes taking part in the game already described, which the two boys and the Jew played regularly every morning. At length he began to languish for the fresh air, and took many occasions of earnestly entreating the old gentleman to allow him to go out to work with his two companions.

Oliver was rendered the more anxious to be actively employed, by what he had seen of the stern morality of the old gentleman's character.

Whenever the Dodger or Charley Bates came home at night empty-handed, he would expatiate with great vehemence on the misery of idle and lazy habits, and enforce upon them the necessity of an active life by sending them supperless to bed. Upon one occasion, indeed, he even went so far as to knock them both down a flight of stairs; but this was carrying out his virtuous precepts to an unusual extent.

At length one morning, Oliver obtained the permission he had so eagerly sought. There had been no handkerchiefs to work upon for two or three days, and the dinners had been rather meagre. Perhaps these were reasons for the old gentleman's giving his assent, but, whether they were or no, he told Oliver he might go, and placed him under the joint guardianship of Charley Bates and his friend the Dodger.

The three boys sallied out: the Dodger with his coat-sleeves tucked up and his hat cocked as usual, Master Bates sauntering along with his hands in his pockets, and Oliver between them, wondering where they were going, and what branch of manufacture he would be instructed in first.

The pace at which they went was such a very lazy, ill-looking saunter, that Oliver soon began to think his companions were going to deceive the old gentleman, by not going to work at all. The Dodger had a vicious propensity, too, of pulling the caps from the heads of small boys and tossing them down areas; while Charley Bates exhibited some very loose notions concerning the rights of property, by pilfering divers apples and onions from the stalls at the kennel sides, and thrusting them into pockets which were so surprisingly capacious, that they seemed to undermine his whole suit of clothes in every direction. These things looked so bad, that Oliver was on the point of declaring his intention of seeking his way back in the best way he could, when his thoughts were suddenly directed into another channel by a very mysterious change of behaviour on the part of the Dodger.

They were just emerging from a narrow court not far from the open square in Clerkenwell, which is yet called, by some strange perversion of terms, "The Green," when the Dodger made a sudden stop, and, laying his finger on his lip, drew his companions back again with the greatest caution and circumspection.

"What's the matter?" demanded Oliver.

"Hush!" replied the Dodger. "Do you see that old cove at the book-stall?"

"The old gentleman over the way?" said Oliver. "Yes, I see him."

"He'll do," said the Dodger.

"A prime plant," observed Charley Bates.

Oliver looked from one to the other with the greatest surprise, but was not permitted to make any inquiries, for the two boys walked stealthily across the road, and slunk close behind the old gentleman towards whom his attention had been directed. Oliver walked a few paces after them, and, not knowing whether to advance or retire, stood looking on in silent amazement.

The old gentleman was a very respectable-looking personage, with a powdered head and gold spectacles; dressed in a bottle-green coat with a black velvet collar, and white trousers, with a smart bamboo cane under his arm. He had taken up a book from the stall, and there he stood, reading away as hard as if he were in his elbow-chair in his own study. It was very possible that he fancied himself there, indeed; for it was plain, from his utter abstraction, that he saw not the book-stall, nor the street, nor the boys, nor, in short, anything but the book itself, which he was reading straight through, turning over the leaves when he got to the bottom of a page, beginning at the top line of the next one, and going regularly on with the greatest interest and eagerness.

What was Oliver's horror and alarm as he stood a few paces off, looking on with his eyelids as wide open as they would possibly go, to see the Dodger plunge his hand into this old gentleman's pocket, and draw from thence a handkerchief which he handed to Charley Bates, and with which they both ran away round the corner at full speed!

In one instant the whole mystery of the handkerchiefs, and the watches, and the jewels,

and the Jew, rushed upon the boy's mind. He stood for a moment with the blood so tingling through all his veins from terror, that he felt as if he were in a burning fire; then, confused and frightened, he took to his heels, and, not knowing what he did, made off as fast as he could lay his feet to the ground.

This was all done in a minute's space, and the very instant that Oliver began to run, the old gentleman putting his hand to his pocket, and missing his handkerchief, turned sharp round. Seeing the boy scudding away at such a rapid pace, he very naturally concluded him to be the depredator, and, shouting "Stop thief!" with all his might, made off after him, book in hand.

But the old gentleman was not the only person who raised the hue-and-cry. The Dodger and Master Bates, unwilling to attract public attention by running down the open street, had merely retired into the very first doorway round the corner. They no sooner heard the cry, and saw Oliver running, than, guessing exactly how the matter stood, they issued forth with great promptitude, and, shouting "Stop thief!" too, joined in the pursuit like good citizens.

Although Oliver had been brought up by philosophers, he was not theoretically acquainted with their beautiful axiom that self-preservation is the first law of nature. If he had been, perhaps he would have been prepared for this. Not being prepared, however, it alarmed him the more; so away he went like the wind, with the old gentleman and the two boys roaring and shouting behind him.

"Stop thief!—stop thief!" There is a magic in the sound. The tradesman leaves his counter, and the carman his waggon; the butcher throws down his tray, the baker his basket, the milk-man his pail, the errand-boy his parcels, the schoolboy his marbles, the paviour his pick-axe, the child his battledore. Away they run, pell-mell, helter-skelter, slap-dash, tearing, yelling, and screaming, knocking down the passengers as they turn the corners, rousing up the dogs, and astonishing the fowls; and streets, squares, and courts re-echo with the sound.

"Stop thief!—stop thief!" The cry is taken up by a hundred voices, and the crowd accumulate at every turning. Away they fly, splashing through the mud, and rattling along the pavements; up go the windows, out run the people, onward bear the mob; a whole audience desert Punch in the very thickest of the plot, and, joining the rushing throng, swell the shout, and lend fresh vigour to the cry, "Stop thief!—stop thief!"

"Stop thief!—stop thief!" There is a passion *for hunting something* deeply implanted in the human breast. One wretched breathless child, panting with exhaustion, terror in his looks, agony in his eye, large drops of perspiration streaming down his face, strains every nerve to make head upon his pursuers; and as they follow on his track, and gain upon him every instant, they hail his decreasing strength with still louder shouts, and whoop and scream with joy "Stop thief!"—Ay, stop him for God's sake, were it only in mercy!

Stopped at last. A clever blow that. He is down upon the pavement, and the crowd eagerly gather round him; each new comer jostling and struggling with the others to catch a glimpse. "Stand aside!"—"Give him a little air!"—"Nonsense! he don't deserve it."—"Where's the gentleman?"—"Here he is, coming down the street."—"Make room there for the gentleman!"—"Is this the boy, sir?"—"Yes."

Oliver lay covered with mud and dust, and bleeding from the mouth, looking wildly round upon the heap of faces that surrounded him, when the old gentleman was officiously dragged and pushed into the circle by the foremost of the pursuers, and made this reply to their anxious inquiries.

"Yes," said the gentleman in a benevolent voice, "I am afraid it is."

"Afraid!" murmured the crowd. "That's a good un."

"Poor fellow!" said the gentleman, "he has hurt himself."

"*I* did that, sir," said a great lubberly fellow, stepping forward; "and preciously I cut my knuckle gain' his mouth. *I* stopped him, sir."

The fellow touched his hat with a grin, expecting something for his pains; but the old gentleman eyeing him with an expression of disgust, looked anxiously round, as if he contemplated running away himself: which it is very possible he might have attempted to do, and thus afforded another chase, had not a police officer (who is generally the last person to arrive in such cases) at that moment made his way through the crowd, and seized Oliver by the collar. " Come, get up," said the man roughly.

" It wasn't me indeed, sir. Indeed, indeed, it was two other boys," said Oliver, clasping his hands passionately, and looking round: " they are here somewhere."

" Oh no, they ain't," said the officer. He meant this to be ironical, but it was true besides, for the Dodger and Charley Bates had filed off down the first convenient court they came to. " Come, get up."

" Don't hurt him," said the old gentleman compassionately.

" Oh no, I won't hurt him," replied the

officer, tearing his jacket half off his back in proof thereof. "Come, I know you; it won't do. Will you stand upon your legs, you young devil?"

Oliver, who could hardly stand, made a shift to raise himself upon his feet, and was at once lugged along the streets by the jacket-collar at a rapid pace. The gentleman walked on with them by the officer's side; and as many of the crowd as could, got a little a-head, and stared back at Oliver from time to time. The boys shouted in triumph, and on they went.

CHAPTER XI.

TREATS OF MR. FANG THE POLICE MAGISTRATE, AND FURNISHES A SLIGHT SPECIMEN OF HIS MODE OF ADMINISTERING JUSTICE.

THE offence had been committed within the district, and indeed in the immediate neighbourhood of a very notorious metropolitan police office. The crowd had only the satisfaction of accompanying Oliver through two or three streets, and down a place called Mutton-hill, when he was led beneath a low arch-way, and up a dirty court into this dispensary of summary justice, by the back way. It was a small paved yard into which they turned; and here they encountered a stout man with a bunch of whiskers on his face, and a bunch of keys in his hand.

"What's the matter now?" said the man carelessly.

"A young fogle-hunter," replied the man who had Oliver in charge.

"Are you the party that's been robbed, sir?" inquired the man with the keys.

"Yes, I am," replied the old gentleman; "but I am not sure that this boy actually took the handkerchief. I—I would rather not press the case."

"Must go before the magistrate now, sir," replied the man. "His worship will be disengaged in half a minute. Now, young gallows."

This was an invitation for Oliver to enter through a door which he unlocked as he spoke, and which led into a stone cell. Here he was searched, and, nothing being found upon him, locked up.

This cell was in shape and size something like an area cellar, only not so light. It was most intolerably dirty, for it was Monday morning, and it had been tenanted by six drunken people, who had been locked up elsewhere since Saturday night. But this is nothing. In our station-houses, men and women are every night confined on the most trivial *charges*—the word is worth noting—in dungeons, compared with which, those in Newgate, occupied by the most atrocious felons, tried, found guilty, and under sentence of death, are palaces. Let any man who doubts this, compare the two.

The old gentleman looked almost as rueful as Oliver when the key grated in the lock; and turned with a sigh to the book which had been the innocent cause of all this disturbance.

" There is something in that boy's face," said the old gentleman to himself as he walked slowly away, tapping his chin with the cover of the book in a thoughtful manner, " something that touches and interests me. *Can* he be innocent? He looked like— By the bye," exclaimed the old gentleman, halting very abruptly, and staring up into the sky, " God bless my soul!—where have I seen something like that look before?"

After musing for some minutes, the old gentleman walked with the same meditative face into a back ante-room opening from the yard; and there, retiring into a corner, called up before his mind's eye a vast amphitheatre of faces over which a dusky curtain had hung for many years. " No," said the old gentleman, shaking his head; " it must be imagination."

He wandered over them again. He had called them into view, and it was not easy to replace the shroud that had so long concealed them. There were the faces of friends and foes, and of many that had been almost strangers, peering intrusively from the crowd ; there were the faces of young and blooming girls that were now old women; there were others that the grave had changed to ghastly trophies of death, but which the mind, superior to his power, still dressed in their old freshness and beauty, calling back the lustre of the eyes, the brightness of the smile, the beaming of the soul through its mask of clay, and whispering of beauty beyond the tomb, changed but to be heightened, and taken from earth only to be set up as a light to shed a soft and gentle glow upon the path to Heaven.

But the old gentleman could recall no one countenance of which Oliver's features bore a trace; so he heaved a sigh over the recollections he had awakened, and being, happily for himself, an absent old gentleman, buried them again in the pages of the musty book.

He was roused by a touch on the shoulder, and a request from the man with the keys to follow him into the office. He closed his book hastily, and was at once ushered into the imposing presence of the renowned Mr. Fang.

The office was a front parlour, with a paneled wall. Mr. Fang sat behind a bar at the upper end; and on one side the door, was a sort of wooden pen in which poor little Oliver was already deposited, trembling very much at the awfulness of the scene.

Mr. Fang was a middle-sized man, with no great quantity of hair, and what he had, growing on the back and sides of his head. His face was stern, and much flushed. If he were really not in the habit of taking rather more than was exactly good for him, he might have brought an action against his countenance for libel, and have recovered heavy damages.

The old gentleman bowed respectfully, and,

advancing to the magistrate's desk, said, suiting the action to the word, " That is my name and address, sir." He then withdrew a pace or two; and, with another polite and gentlemanly inclination of the head, waited to be questioned.

Now, it so happened that Mr. Fang was at that moment perusing a leading article in a newspaper of the morning, adverting to some recent decision of his, and commending him, for the three hundred and fiftieth time, to the special and particular notice of the Secretary of State for the Home Department. He was out of temper, and he looked up with an angry scowl.

" Who are you?" said Mr. Fang.

The old gentleman pointed with some surprise to his card.

" Officer!" said Mr. Fang, tossing the card contemptuously away with the newspaper, " who is this fellow?"

" My name, sir," said the old gentleman, speaking *like* a gentleman,—" my name, sir, is Brownlow. Permit me to inquire the name of the magistrate who offers a gratuitous and unprovoked insult to a respectable man, under the protection of the bench." Saying this, Mr. Brownlow looked round the office as if in search of some person who would afford him the required information.

"Officer!" said Mr. Fang, throwing the paper on one side, "what's this fellow charged with?"

"He's not charged at all, your worship," replied the officer. "He appears against the boy, your worship."

His worship knew this perfectly well; but it was a good annoyance, and a safe one.

"Appears against the boy, does he?" said Fang, surveying Mr. Brownlow contemptuously from head to foot. "Swear him!"

"Before I am sworn I must beg to say one word," said Mr. Brownlow; "and that is, that I never, without actual experience, could have believed——"

"Hold your tongue, sir!" said Mr. Fang peremptorily.

"I will not, sir!" replied the old gentleman.

"Hold your tongue this instant, or I'll have you turned out of the office!" said Mr. Fang. "You're an insolent, impertinent fellow. How dare you bully a magistrate!"

"What!" exclaimed the old gentleman, reddening.

"Swear this person!" said Fang to the clerk. "I'll not hear another word. Swear him."

Mr. Brownlow's indignation was greatly roused; but, reflecting that he might only injure the boy by giving vent to it, he suppressed his feelings, and submitted to be sworn at once.

"Now," said Fang, "what's the charge against this boy? What have you got to say, sir?"

"I was standing at a book-stall—" Mr. Brownlow began.

"Hold your tongue, sir!" said Mr. Fang. "Policeman!—where's the policeman? Here, swear this man. Now, policeman, what is this?"

The policeman with becoming humility related how he had taken the charge, how he had searched Oliver, and found nothing on his person; and how that was all he knew about it.

"Are there any witnesses?" inquired Mr. Fang.

"None, your worship," replied the policeman.

Mr. Fang sat silent for some minutes, and then, turning round to the prosecutor, said in a towering passion,

"Do you mean to state what your complaint against this boy is, fellow, or do you not? You have been sworn. Now, if you stand there, refusing to give evidence, I'll punish you for disrespect to the bench; I will, by——"

By what or by whom, nobody knows, for the clerk and jailer coughed very loud just at the right moment, and the former dropped a heavy book upon the floor; thus preventing the word from being heard—accidentally, of course.

With many interruptions, and repeated insults, Mr. Brownlow contrived to state his case; observing that, in the surprise of the moment, he had run after the boy because he saw him running away, and expressing his hope that, if the magistrate should believe him, although not actually the thief, to be connected with thieves, he would deal as leniently with him as justice would allow.

"He has been hurt already," said the old gentleman in conclusion. "And I fear," he added, with great energy, looking towards the bar,—"I really fear that he is very ill."

"Oh! yes; I dare say!" said Mr. Fang, with a sneer. "Come; none of your tricks here, you young vagabond; they won't do. What's your name?"

Oliver tried to reply, but his tongue failed him. He was deadly pale, and the whole place seemed turning round and round.

"What's your name, you hardened scoundrel?" thundered Mr. Fang. "Officer, what's his name?"

This was addressed to a bluff old fellow in a striped waistcoat, who was standing by the bar. He bent over Oliver, and repeated the inquiry; but finding him really incapable of understanding the question, and knowing that his not replying would only infuriate the magistrate the more, and add to the severity of his sentence, he hazarded a guess.

"He says his name's Tom White, your worship," said this kind-hearted thief-taker.

"Oh, he won't speak out, won't he?" said Fang. "Very well, very well. Where does he live?"

"Where he can, your worship," replied the officer, again pretending to receive Oliver's answer.

"Has he any parents?" inquired Mr. Fang.

"He says they died in his infancy, your worship," replied the officer, hazarding the usual reply.

At this point of the inquiry Oliver raised his head, and, looking round with imploring eyes, murmured a feeble prayer for a draught of water.

"Stuff and nonsense!" said Mr. Fang; "don't try to make a fool of me."

"I think he really is ill, your worship," remonstrated the officer.

"I know better," said Mr. Fang.

"Take care of him, officer," said the old gentleman, raising his hands instinctively; "he'll fall down."

"Stand away, officer," cried Fang savagely; "let him if he likes."

Oliver availed himself of the kind permission, and fell heavily to the floor in a fainting fit. The men in the office looked at each other, but no one dared to stir.

"I knew he was shamming," said Fang, as if this were incontestable proof of the fact. "Let him lie; he'll soon be tired of that."

"How do you propose to deal with the case, sir?" inquired the clerk in a low voice.

"Summarily," replied Mr. Fang. "He stands committed for three months,—hard labour of course. Clear the office."

The door was opened for this purpose, and a couple of men were preparing to carry the insensible boy to his cell, when an elderly man of decent but poor appearance, clad in an old suit of black, rushed hastily into the office, and advanced to the bench.

"Stop, stop,—don't take him away,—for

Heaven's sake stop a moment," cried the new-comer, breathless with haste.

Although the presiding geniuses in such an office as this, exercise a summary and arbitrary power over the liberties, the good name, the character, almost the lives of Her Majesty's subjects, especially of the poorer class; and although within such walls enough fantastic tricks are daily played to make the angels weep hot tears of blood, they are closed to the public, save through the medium of the daily press. Mr. Fang was consequently not a little indignant to see an unbidden guest enter in such irreverent disorder.

"What is this?—who is this? Turn this man out. Clear the office," cried Mr. Fang.

"I will speak," cried the man; "I will not be turned out,—I saw it all. I keep the bookstall. I demand to be sworn. I will not be put down. Mr. Fang, you must hear me. You dare not refuse, sir."

The man was right. His manner was bold and determined, and the matter was growing rather too serious to be hushed up.

"Swear the fellow," growled Fang with a very ill grace. "Now, man, what have you got to say?"

"This," said the man: "I saw three boys—two others and the prisoner here—loitering on the opposite side of the way, when this gentleman was reading. The robbery was committed by another boy. I saw it done, and I saw that this boy was perfectly amazed and stupified by it." Having by this time recovered a little breath, the worthy book-stall keeper proceeded to relate in a more coherent manner the exact circumstances of the robbery.

"Why didn't you come here before?" said Fang after a pause.

"I hadn't a soul to mind the shop," replied the man; "everybody that could have helped me had joined in the pursuit. I could get nobody till five minutes ago, and I've run here all the way."

"The prosecutor was reading, was he?" inquired Fang, after another pause.

"Yes," replied the man, "the very book he has in his hand."

"Oh, that book, eh?" said Fang. "Is it paid for?"

"No, it is not," replied the man, with a smile.

"Dear me, I forgot all about it!" exclaimed the absent old gentleman, innocently.

"A nice person to prefer a charge against a poor boy!" said Fang, with a comical effort to look humane. "I consider, sir, that you have obtained possession of that book under very suspicious and disreputable circumstances, and you may think yourself very fortunate that the owner of the property declines to prosecute. Let this be a lesson to you, my man, or the law will overtake you yet. The boy is discharged. Clear the office!"

"D—n me!" cried the old gentleman, bursting out with the rage he had kept down so long, "d—me! I'll——"

"Clear the office!" roared the magistrate. "Officers, do you hear? Clear the office!"

The mandate was obeyed, and the indignant Mr. Brownlow was conveyed out, with the book in one hand and the bamboo cane in the other in a perfect phrenzy of rage and defiance.

He reached the yard, and it vanished in a moment. Little Oliver Twist lay on his back on the pavement, with his shirt unbuttoned and his temples bathed with water; his face a deadly white, and a cold tremble convulsing his whole frame.

"Poor boy, poor boy!" said Mr. Brownlow, bending over him. "Call a coach, somebody, pray,—directly!"

A coach was obtained, and Oliver, having been carefully laid on one seat, the old gentleman got in and sat himself on the other.

"May I accompany you?" said the book-stall keeper, looking in.

"Bless me, yes, my dear friend," said Mr. Brownlow quickly. "I forgot you. Dear, dear! I have this unhappy book still. Jump in. Poor fellow! there's no time to lose."

The book-stall keeper got into the coach, and away they drove.

CHAPTER XII.

IN WHICH OLIVER IS TAKEN BETTER CARE OF THAN HE EVER WAS BEFORE. WITH SOME PARTICULARS CONCERNING A CERTAIN PICTURE.

THE coach rattled away down Mount Pleasant and up Exmouth-street,—over nearly the same ground as that which Oliver had traversed when he first entered London in company with the Dodger, — and, turning a different way when it reached the Angel at Islington, stopped at length before a neat house in a quiet shady street near Pentonville. Here a bed was prepared without loss of time, in which Mr. Brownlow saw his young charge carefully and comfortably deposited; and here he was tended with a kindness and solicitude which knew no bounds.

But for many days Oliver remained insensible

to all the goodness of his new friends; the sun rose and sunk, and rose and sunk again, and many times after that, and still the boy lay stretched upon his uneasy bed, dwindling away beneath the dry and wasting heat of fever,— that heat which, like the subtle acid that gnaws into the very heart of hardest iron, burns only to corrode and to destroy. The worm does not his work more surely on the dead body, than does this slow creeping fire upon the living frame.

Weak, and thin, and pallid, he awoke at last from what seemed to have been a long and troubled dream. Feebly raising himself in the bed, with his head resting on his trembling arm, he looked anxiously round.

"What room is this?—where have I been brought to?" said Oliver. "This is not the place I went to sleep in."

He uttered these words in a feeble voice, being very faint and weak; but they were overheard at once, for the curtain at the bed's head was hastily drawn back, and a motherly old lady, very neatly and precisely dressed, rose as she undrew it, from an arm-chair close by, in which she had been sitting at needle-work.

"Hush, my dear," said the old lady softly. "You must be very quiet, or you will be ill again, and you have been very bad,—as bad as bad could be, pretty nigh. Lie down again—there's a dear." With these words the old lady very gently placed Oliver's head upon the pillow, and, smoothing back his hair from his forehead, looked so kindly and lovingly in his face, that he could not help placing his little withered hand upon hers, and drawing it round his neck.

"Save us!" said the old lady, with tears in her eyes, "what a grateful little dear it is. Pretty creetur! what would his mother feel if she had sat by him as I have, and could see him now!"

"Perhaps she does see me," whispered Oliver, folding his hands together; "perhaps she has sat by me, ma'am. I almost feel as if she had."

"That was the fever, my dear," said the old lady mildly.

"I suppose it was," replied Oliver thoughtfully, " because heaven is a long way off, and they are too happy there to come down to the bedside of a poor boy. But if she knew I was ill, she must have pitied me even there, for she was very ill herself before she died. She can't know anything about me though," added Oliver after a moment's silence, " for if she had seen me beat, it would have made her sorrowful; and her face has always looked sweet and happy when I have dreamt of her."

The old lady made no reply to this, but wiping her eyes first, and her spectacles, which lay on the counterpane, afterwards, as if they were part and parcel of those features, brought some cool stuff for Oliver to drink, and then patting him on the cheek, told him he must lie very quiet, or he would be ill again.

So Oliver kept very still, partly because he was anxious to obey the kind old lady in all things, and partly, to tell the truth, because he was completely exhausted with what he had already said. He soon fell into a gentle doze, from which he was awakened by the light of a candle, which, being brought near the bed, showed him a gentleman, with a very large and loud-ticking gold watch in his hand, who felt his pulse and said he was a great deal better.

"You *are* a great deal better, are you not, my dear?" said the gentleman.

"Yes, thank you, sir," replied Oliver.

"Yes, I know you are," said the gentleman: "You're hungry too, an't you?"

"No, sir," answered Oliver.

"Hem!" said the gentleman. "No, I know you're not. He is not hungry, Mrs. Bedwin," said the gentleman, looking very wise.

The old lady made a respectful inclination of the head, which seemed to say that she thought the doctor was a very clever man. The doctor appeared very much of the same opinion himself.

"You feel sleepy, don't you, my dear?" said the doctor.

"No, sir," replied Oliver.

"No," said the doctor with a very shrewd and satisfied look. "You're not sleepy. Nor thirsty, are you?"

"Yes, sir, rather thirsty," answered Oliver.

"Just as I expected, Mrs. Bedwin," said the doctor. "It's very natural that he should be thirsty—perfectly natural. You may give him a little tea, ma'am, and some dry toast without any butter. Don't keep him too warm, ma'am; but be careful that you don't let him be too cold—will you have the goodness?"

The old lady dropped a curtsey; and the doctor, after tasting the cool stuff, and expressing a qualified approval thereof, hurried away: his boots creaking in a very important and wealthy manner as he went down stairs.

Oliver dozed off again soon after this, and when he awoke it was nearly twelve o'clock. The old lady tenderly bade him good-night shortly afterwards, and left him in charge of a fat old woman who had just come, bringing with her in a little bundle a small Prayer Book and a large nightcap. Putting the latter on her head, and the former on the table, the old woman, after telling Oliver that she had come to sit up with him, drew her chair close to the fire and went off into a series of short naps, chequered at frequent intervals with sundry tumblings forward, and divers moans and chokings, which, however, had no worse effect than causing her to rub her nose very hard, and then fall asleep again.

And thus the night crept slowly on. Oliver lay awake for some time, counting the little circles of light which the reflection of the rushlight-shade threw upon the ceiling, or tracing with his languid eyes the intricate pattern of the paper on the wall. The darkness and deep stillness of the room were very solemn; and as they brought into the boy's mind the thought that death had been hovering there for many days and nights, and might yet fill it with the gloom and dread of his awful presence, he turned his face upon the pillow, and fervently prayed to Heaven.

Gradually he fell into that deep tranquil sleep which ease from recent suffering alone imparts; that calm and peaceful rest which it is pain to wake from. Who, if this were death, would be roused again to all the struggles and turmoils of life,—to all its cares for the present, its anxieties for the future, and, more than all, its weary recollections of the past!

It had been bright day for hours when Oliver opened his eyes, and when he did so, he felt cheerful and happy. The crisis of the disease was safely past, and he belonged to the world again.

In three days' time he was able to sit in an easy-chair well propped up with pillows; and, as he was still too weak to walk, Mrs. Bedwin had him carried down stairs into the little house-keeper's room, which belonged to her, where having sat him up by the fireside, the good old lady sat herself down too, and, being in a state of considerable delight at seeing him so much better, forthwith began to cry most violently.

"Never mind me, my dear," said the old lady; "I'm only having a regular good cry. There; it's all over now, and I'm quite comfortable."

"You're very, very kind to me, ma'am," said Oliver.

"Well, never you mind that, my dear," said

the old lady; "that's got nothing to do with your broth, and it's full time you had it, for the doctor says Mr. Brownlow may come in to see you this morning, and we must get up our best looks, because the better we look the more he'll be pleased." And with this, the old lady applied herself to warming up in a little saucepan a basin full of broth, strong enough to furnish an ample dinner, when reduced to the regulation strength, for three hundred and fifty paupers, at the very lowest computation.

"Are you fond of pictures, dear?" inquired the old lady, seeing that Oliver had fixed his eyes most intently on a portrait which hung against the wall just opposite his chair.

"I don't quite know, ma'am," said Oliver, without taking his eyes from the canvass; "I have seen so few that I hardly know. What a beautiful, mild face that lady's is!"

"Ah!" said the old lady, "painters always make ladies out prettier than they are, or they wouldn't get any custom, child. The man that invented the machine for taking likenesses might have known *that* would never succeed; it's a deal too honest,—a deal," said the old lady, laughing very heartily at her own acuteness.

"Is—is that a likeness, ma'am?" said Oliver.

"Yes," said the old lady, looking up for a moment from the broth: "that's a portrait."

"Whose, ma'am?" asked Oliver eagerly.

"Why, really, my dear, I don't know," answered the old lady in a good-humoured manner. "It's not a likeness of anybody that you or I know, I expect. It seems to strike your fancy, dear."

"It is so very pretty—so very beautiful," replied Oliver.

"Why, sure you're not afraid of it?" said the old lady, observing in great surprise the look of awe with which the child regarded the painting.

"Oh no, no," returned Oliver quickly; "but the eyes look so sorrowful, and where I sit they seem fixed upon me. It makes my heart beat," added Oliver in a low voice, "as if it was alive, and wanted to speak to me, but couldn't."

"Lord save us!" exclaimed the old lady, starting; "don't talk in that way, child. You're weak and nervous after your illness. Let me wheel your chair round to the other side, and then you won't see it. There," said the old lady, suiting the action to the word; "you don't see it now, at all events."

Oliver *did* see it in his mind's eye as distinctly as if he had not altered his position, but he thought it better not to worry the kind old lady; so he smiled gently when she looked at him, and Mrs. Bedwin, satisfied that he felt more comfortable, salted and broke bits of toasted bread into the broth with all the bustle befitting so solemn a preparation. Oliver got through it with extraordinary expedition, and had scarcely swallowed the last spoonful when there came a soft tap at the door. "Come in," said the old lady; and in walked Mr. Brownlow.

Now, the old gentleman came in as brisk as need be; but he had no sooner raised his spectacles on his forehead, and thrust his hands behind the skirts of his dressing-gown to take a good long look at Oliver, than his countenance underwent a very great variety of odd contortions. Oliver looked very worn and shadowy from sickness, and made an ineffectual attempt to stand up, out of respect to his benefactor, which terminated in his sinking back into the chair again; and the fact is, if the truth must be told, that Mr. Brownlow's heart being large enough for any six ordinary old gentlemen of humane disposition, forced a supply of tears into his eyes by some hydraulic process which we are not sufficiently philosophical to be in a condition to explain.

"Poor boy, poor boy!" said Mr. Brownlow, clearing his throat. "I'm rather hoarse this morning, Mrs. Bedwin; I'm afraid I have caught cold."

"I hope not, sir," said Mrs. Bedwin. "Everything you have had, has been well aired, sir."

"I don't know, Bedwin,—I don't know," said Mr. Brownlow; "I rather think I had a damp napkin at dinner-time yesterday: but never mind that. How do you feel, my dear?"

"Very happy, sir," replied Oliver, "and very grateful indeed, sir, for your goodness to me."

"Good boy," said Mr. Brownlow stoutly. "Have you given him any nourishment, Bedwin?—any slops, eh?"

"He has just had a basin of beautiful strong broth, sir," replied Mrs. Bedwin, drawing herself up slightly, and laying a strong emphasis on the last word, to intimate that between slops, and broth well compounded, there existed no affinity or connexion whatsoever.

"Ugh!" said Mr. Brownlow, with a slight shudder; "a couple of glasses of port wine would have done him a great deal more good,—wouldn't they, Tom White,—eh?"

"My name is Oliver, sir," replied the little invalid with a look of great astonishment.

"Oliver," said Mr. Brownlow; "Oliver what? Oliver White,—eh?"

"No, sir, Twist,—Oliver Twist."

"Queer name," said the old gentleman. "What made you tell the magistrate your name was White?"

"I never told him so, sir," returned Oliver in amazement.

This sounded so like a falsehood, that the old gentleman looked somewhat sternly in Oliver's face. It was impossible to doubt him; there was truth in every one of its thin and sharpened lineaments.

"Some mistake," said Mr. Brownlow. But, although his motive for looking steadily at Oliver no longer existed, the old idea of the resemblance between his features and some familiar face came upon him so strongly that he could not withdraw his gaze.

"I hope you are not angry with me, sir?" said Oliver, raising his eyes beseechingly.

"No, no," replied the old gentleman.— "Gracious God, what's this!—Bedwin, look, look there!"

As he spoke, he pointed hastily to the picture above Oliver's head, and then to the boy's face. There was its living copy,—the eyes, the head, the mouth; every feature was the same. The expression was for the instant so precisely alike, that the minutest line seemed copied with an accuracy which was perfectly unearthly.

Oliver knew not the cause of this sudden exclamation, for he was not strong enough to bear the start it gave him, and he fainted away.

CHAPTER XIII.

REVERTS TO THE MERRY OLD GENTLEMAN AND HIS YOUTHFUL FRIENDS, THROUGH WHOM A NEW ACQUAINTANCE IS INTRODUCED TO THE INTELLIGENT READER, AND CONNECTED WITH WHOM VARIOUS PLEASANT MATTERS ARE RELATED APPERTAINING TO THIS HISTORY.

When the Dodger and his accomplished friend Master Bates joined in the hue-and-cry which was raised at Oliver's heels, in consequence of their executing an illegal conveyance of Mr. Brownlow's personal property, as has been already described with great perspicuity in a foregoing chapter, they were actuated, as we therein took occasion to observe, by a very laudable and becoming regard for themselves: and forasmuch as the freedom of the subject and the liberty of the individual are among the first and proudest boasts of a true-hearted Englishman, so I need hardly beg the reader to observe that this action must tend to exalt them in the opinion of all public and patriotic men, in almost as great a degree as this strong proof of their anxiety for their own preservation and safety goes to corroborate and confirm the little code of laws which certain profound and sound-judging philosophers have laid down as the mainsprings of all Nature's deeds and actions; the said philosophers very wisely reducing the good lady's proceedings to matters of maxim and theory, and by a very neat and pretty compliment to her exalted wisdom and understanding, putting entirely out of sight any considerations of heart, or generous impulse and feeling, as matters totally beneath a female who is acknowledged by universal admission to be so far beyond the numerous little foibles and weaknesses of her sex.

If I wanted any further proof of the strictly philosophical nature of the conduct of these young gentlemen in their very delicate predicament, I should at once find it in the fact (also recorded in a foregoing part of this narrative) of their quitting the pursuit when the general attention was fixed upon Oliver, and making immediately for their home by the shortest possible cut; for although I do not mean to assert that it is the practice of renowned and learned sages at all to shorten the road to any great conclusion, their course indeed being rather to lengthen the distance by various circumlocutions and discursive staggerings, like unto those in which drunken men under the pressure of a too mighty flow of ideas are prone to indulge, still I do mean to say, and do say distinctly, that it is the invariable practice of all mighty philosophers, in carrying out their theories, to evince great wisdom and foresight in providing against every possible contingency which can be supposed at all likely to affect themselves. Thus, to do a great right, you may do a little wrong, and you may take any means which the end to be attained will justify; the amount of the right or the amount of the wrong, or indeed the distinction between the two, being left entirely to the philosopher concerned: to be settled and determined by his clear, comprehensive, and impartial view of his own particular case.

It was not until the two boys had scoured with great rapidity through a most intricate maze of narrow streets and courts, that they ventured to halt by one consent beneath a low and dark archway. Having remained silent here, just long enough to recover breath to speak, Master Bates uttered an exclamation of amusement and delight, and, bursting into an uncontrollable fit of laughter, flung himself upon a door-step, and rolled thereon in a transport of mirth.

"What's the matter?" inquired the Dodger.

"Ha! ha! ha!" roared Charley Bates.

"Hold your noise," remonstrated the Dodger, looking cautiously round. "Do you want to be grabbed, stupid?"

"I can't help it," said Charley, "I can't help it. To see him splitting away at that pace, and cutting round the corners, and knocking up against the posts, and starting on again as if he was made of iron as well as them, and me with the wipe in my pocket, singing out arter him—oh, my eye!" The vivid imagination of Master Bates presented the scene before him in too strong colours. As he arrived at this apostrophe, he again rolled upon the doorstep, and laughed louder than before.

"What'll Fagin say?" inquired the Dodger, taking advantage of the next interval of breathlessness on the part of his friend to propound the question.

"What!" repeated Charley Bates.

"Ah, what?" said the Dodger.

"Why, what should he say?" inquired Charley, stopping rather suddenly in his merriment, for the Dodger's manner was impressive; "what should he say?"

Mr. Dawkins whistled for a couple of minutes, and then, taking off his hat, scratched his head and nodded thrice.

"What do you mean?" said Charley.

"Toor rul lol loo, gammon and spinnage, the frog he wouldn't, and high cockolorum," said the Dodger, with a slight sneer on his intellectual countenance.

This was explanatory, but not satisfactory.

Master Bates felt it so, and again said, "What do you mean?"

The Dodger made no reply, but putting his hat on again, and gathering the skirts of his long-tailed coat under his arms, thrust his tongue into his cheek, slapped the bridge of his nose some half-dozen times in a familiar but expressive manner, and turning on his heel, slunk down the court. Master Bates followed, with a thoughtful countenance. The noise of footsteps on the creaking stairs a few minutes after the occurrence of this conversation roused the merry old gentleman as he sat over the fire with a saveloy and a small loaf in his left hand, a pocket knife in his right, and a pewter pot on the trivet. There was a rascally smile on his white face as he turned round, and, looking sharply out from under his thick red eyebrows, bent his ear towards the door and listened intently.

"Why, how's this?" muttered the Jew, changing countenance; "only two of 'em! Where's the third? They can't have got into trouble. Hark!"

The footsteps approached nearer; they reached the landing, the door was slowly opened, and the Dodger and Charley Bates entered and closed it behind them.

"Where's Oliver?" said the furious Jew, rising with a menacing look: "where's the boy?"

The young thieves eyed their preceptor as if they were alarmed at his violence, and looked uneasily at each other, but made no reply.

"What's become of the boy?" said the Jew, seizing the Dodger tightly by the collar, and threatening him with horrid imprecations. "Speak out, or I'll throttle you!"

Mr. Fagin looked so very much in earnest, that Charley Bates, who deemed it prudent in all cases to be on the safe side, and conceived it by no means improbable that it might be his turn to be throttled second, dropped upon his knees, and raised a loud, well-sustained, and continuous roar, something between an insane bull and a speaking-trumpet.

"Will you speak?" thundered the Jew, shaking the Dodger so much that his keeping in the big coat at all seemed perfectly miraculous.

"Why, the traps have got him, and that's all about it," said the Dodger sullenly. "Come, let go o' me, will you!" and, swinging himself at one jerk clean out of the big coat, which he left in the Jew's hands, the Dodger snatched up the toasting-fork and made a pass at the merry old gentleman's waistcoat, which, if it had taken effect, would have let a little more merriment out than could have been easily replaced in a month or two.

The Jew stepped back in this emergency with more agility than could have been anticipated in a man of his apparent decrepitude, and, seizing up the pot, prepared to hurl it at his assailant's head. But Charley Bates at this moment calling his attention by a perfectly terrific howl, he suddenly altered its destination, and flung it full at that young gentleman.

"Why, what the blazes is in the wind now!" growled a deep voice. "Who pitched that 'ere at me? It's well it's the beer, and not the pot, as hit me, or I'd have settled somebody. I might have know'd, as nobody but an infernal, rich, plundering, thundering old Jew could afford to throw away any drink but water, and not that, unless he done the River company every quarter. Wot's it all about, Fagin? D—me, if my neckankecher an't lined with beer. Come in, you sneaking warmint; wot are you stopping outside for, as if you was ashamed of your master. Come in!"

The man who growled out these words was a stoutly-built fellow of about five-and-thirty, in a black velveteen coat, very soiled drab breeches, lace-up half-boots, and grey cotton stockings, which enclosed a very bulky pair of legs, with large swelling calves,—the kind of legs which in such costume always look in an unfinished and incomplete state without a set of fetters to garnish them. He had a brown hat on his head, and a dirty belcher handkerchief round his neck, with the long frayed ends of which he smeared the beer from his face as he spoke: disclosing, when he had done so, a broad heavy countenance with a beard of three days' growth, and two scowling eyes, one of which displayed various parti-coloured symptoms of having been recently damaged by a blow.

"Come in, d'ye hear?" growled this engaging-looking ruffian. A white shaggy dog, with his face scratched and torn in twenty different places, skulked into the room.

"Why didn't you come in afore?" said the man. "You're getting too proud to own me afore company, are you? Lie down!"

This command was accompanied with a kick which sent the animal to the other end of the room. He appeared well used to it, however; for he coiled himself up in a corner, very quietly without uttering a sound, and, winking his very ill-looking eyes about twenty times in a minute, appeared to occupy himself in taking a survey of the apartment.

"What are you up to? Ill-treating the boys, you covetous, avaricious in-sa-ti-a-ble old fence?" said the man, seating himself deliberately. "I wonder they don't murder you; *I* would if I was them. If I'd been your 'prentice, I'd have done it long ago; and—no, I couldn't have sold you arterwards, though; for you 're fit for nothing but keeping as a curiosity of ugliness in a glass bottle, and I suppose they don't blow them large enough."

"Hush! hush! Mr. Sikes," said the Jew, trembling; "don't speak so loud."

"None of your mistering," replied the ruffian; "you always mean mischief when you come that. You know my name: out with it. I shan't disgrace it when the time comes."

"Well, well, then—Bill Sikes," said the Jew with abject humility. "You seem out of humour, Bill."

"Perhaps I am," replied Sikes. "I should think *you* were rather out of sorts too, unless you mean as little harm when you throw pewter pots about, as you do when you blab and ——"

"Are you mad?" said the Jew, catching the man by the sleeve, and pointing towards the boys.

Mr. Sikes contented himself with tying an imaginary knot under his left ear, and jerking his head over on the right shoulder; a piece of dumb show which the Jew appeared to understand perfectly. He then in cant terms, with which his whole conversation was plentifully besprinkled, but which would be quite unintelligible if they were recorded here, demanded a glass of liquor.

"And mind you don't poison it," said Mr. Sikes, laying his hat upon the table.

This was said in jest; but if the speaker could have seen the evil leer with which the Jew bit his pale lip as he turned round to the cupboard, he might have thought the caution not wholly unnecessary, or the wish (at all events,) to improve upon the distiller's ingenuity not very far from the old gentleman's merry heart.

After swallowing two or three glassfulls of spirits, Mr. Sikes condescended to take some notice of the young gentlemen; which gracious act led to a conversation in which the cause and manner of Oliver's capture were circumstantially detailed, with such alterations and improvements on the truth as to the Dodger appeared most advisable under the circumstances.

"I'm afraid," said the Jew, "that he may say something which will get us into trouble."

"That's very likely," returned Sikes with a malicious grin. "You're blowed upon, Fagin."

"And I'm afraid, you see," added the Jew, speaking as if he had not noticed the interruption, and regarding the other closely as he did so,—"I'm afraid that, if the game was up with us, it might be up with a good many more; and that it would come out rather worse for you than it would for me, my dear."

The man started, and turned fiercely round upon the Jew; but the old gentleman's shoulders were shrugged up to his ears, and his eyes were vacantly staring on the opposite wall.

There was a long pause. Every member of the respectable coterie appeared plunged in his own reflections, not excepting the dog, who by a certain malicious licking of his lips seemed to be meditating an attack upon the legs of the first gentleman or lady he might encounter in the streets when he went out.

"Somebody must find out what's been done

at the office," said Mr. Sikes in a much lower tone than he had taken since he came in.

The Jew nodded assent.

"If he hasn't peached, and is committed, there's no fear till he comes out again," said Mr. Sikes, "and then he must be taken care on. You must get hold of him, somehow."

Again the Jew nodded.

The prudence of this line of action, indeed, was obvious, but unfortunately there was one very strong objection to its being adopted; and this was, that the Dodger, and Charley Bates, and Fagin, and Mr. William Sikes, happened one and all to entertain a most violent and deeply-rooted antipathy to going near a police-office on any ground or pretext whatever.

How long they might have sat and looked at each other in a state of uncertainty not the most pleasant of its kind, it is difficult to say. It is not necessary to make any guesses on the subject, however; for the sudden entrance of the two young ladies whom Oliver had seen on a former occasion caused the conversation to flow afresh.

"The very thing!" said the Jew. "Bet will go; won't you, my dear?"

"Wheres?" inquired the young lady.

"Only just up to the office, my dear," said the Jew coaxingly.

It is due to the young lady to say that she did not positively affirm that she would not, but that she merely expressed an emphatic and earnest desire to be "blessed" if she would; a polite and delicate evasion of the request, which shows the young lady to have been possessed of that natural good-breeding which cannot bear to inflict upon a fellow-creature the pain of a direct and pointed refusal.

The Jew's countenance fell, and he turned from this young lady, who was gaily, not to say gorgeously attired, in a red gown, green boots, and yellow curl-papers, to the other female.

"Nancy, my dear," said the Jew in a soothing manner, "what do *you* say?"

"That it won't do; so it's no use a-trying it on, Fagin," replied Nancy.

"What do you mean by that?" said Mr. Sikes, looking up in a surly manner.

"What I say, Bill," replied the lady collectedly.

"Why, you're just the very person for it," reasoned Mr. Sikes: "nobody about here knows anything of you."

"And as I don't want 'em to, neither," replied Nancy in the same composed manner, "it's rather more no than yes with me, Bill."

"She'll go, Fagin," said Sikes.

"No, she won't, Fagin," bawled Nancy.

"Yes, she will, Fagin," said Sikes.

And Mr. Sikes was right. By dint of alternate threats, promises, and bribes, the female in question was ultimately prevailed upon to undertake the commission. She was not indeed withheld by the same considerations as her agreeable friend, for having very recently removed into the neighbourhood of Field-lane from the remote but genteel suburb of Ratcliffe, she was not under the same apprehension of being recognised by any of her numerous acquaintance.

Accordingly, with a clean white apron tied

over her gown, and her curl-papers tucked up under a straw bonnet,—both articles of dress being provided from the Jew's inexhaustible stock,—Miss Nancy prepared to issue forth on her errand.

"Stop a minute, my dear," said the Jew, producing a little covered basket. "Carry that in one hand; it looks more respectable, my dear."

"Give her a door-key to carry in her t'other one, Fagin," said Sikes; "it looks real and genivine like."

"Yes, yes, my dear, so it does," said the Jew, hanging a large street-door key on the fore-finger of the young lady's right hand. "There; very good,—very good indeed, my dear," said the Jew, rubbing his hands.

"Oh, my brother! my poor, dear, sweet, innocent little brother!" exclaimed Nancy, bursting into tears, and wringing the little basket and the street-door key in an agony of distress. "What has become of him!—where have they taken him to! Oh, do have pity, and tell me what's been done with the dear boy, gentlemen; do, gentlemen, if you please, gentlemen."

Having uttered these words in a most lamentable and heart-broken tone, to the immeasurable delight of her hearers, Miss Nancy paused, winked to the company, nodded smilingly round, and disappeared.

" Ah! she's a clever girl, my dears," said the Jew, turning round to his young friends, and shaking his head gravely, as if in mute admonition to them to follow the bright example they had just beheld.

She's a honour to her sex," said Mr. Sikes, filling his glass, and smiting the table with his enormous fist. " Here's her health, and wishing they was all like her!"

While these and many other encomiums were being passed on the accomplished Nancy, that young lady made the best of her way to the police-office; whither, notwithstanding a little natural timidity consequent upon walking through the streets alone and unprotected, she arrived in perfect safety shortly afterwards.

Entering by the back way, she tapped softly

with the key at one of the cell-doors, and listened. There was no sound within, so she coughed and listened again. Still there was no reply, so she spoke.

" Nolly, dear?" murmured Nancy in a gentle voice;—" Nolly?"

There was nobody inside but a miserable shoeless criminal, who had been taken up for playing the flute, and who—the offence against society having been clearly proved—had been very properly committed by Mr. Fang to the House of Correction for one month, with the appropriate and amusing remark that since he had so much breath to spare, it would be much more wholesomely expended on the treadmill than in a musical instrument. He made no answer, being occupied in mentally bewailing the loss of the flute, which had been confiscated for the use of the county; so Nancy passed on to the next cell, and knocked there.

" Well," cried a faint and feeble voice.

" Is there a little boy here?" inquired Nancy with a preliminary sob.

" No," replied the voice; " God forbid!"

This was a vagrant of sixty-five, who was going to prison for *not* playing the flute, or, in other words, for begging in the streets, and doing nothing for his livelihood. In the next cell was another man, who was going to the same prison for hawking tin saucepans without a licence: thereby doing something for his living in defiance of the Stamp-office.

But, as neither of these criminals answered to the name of Oliver, or knew anything about him, Nancy made straight up to the bluff officer in the striped waistcoat, and with the most piteous wailings and lamentations, rendered more piteous by a prompt and efficient use of the street-door key and the little basket, demanded her own dear brother.

"I haven't got him, my dear," said the old man.

"Where is he?" screamed Nancy in a distracted manner.

"Why, the gentleman's got him," replied the officer.

"What gentleman?—Oh, gracious heavens! what gentleman?" exclaimed Nancy.

In reply to this incoherent questioning, the old man informed the deeply affected sister that Oliver had been taken ill in the office, and discharged in consequence of a witness having proved the robbery to have been committed by another boy not in custody; and that the prosecutor had carried him away in an insensible condition to his own residence, of and concerning which all the informant knew was, that it was somewhere at Pentonville; he having heard that word mentioned in the directions to the coachman.

In a dreadful state of doubt and uncertainty the agonised young woman staggered to the gate, and then,—exchanging her faltering gait for a good swift steady run, returned by the most devious and complicated route she could think of, to the domicile of the Jew.

Mr. Bill Sikes no sooner heard the account of the expedition delivered, than he very hastily called up the white dog, and, putting on his hat, expeditiously departed, without devoting any time to the formality of wishing the company good-morning.

"We must know where he is, my dears; he must be found," said the Jew, greatly excited. "Charley, do nothing but skulk about, till you bring home some news of him. Nancy, my dear, I must have him found: I trust to you, my dear,—to you and the Artful for everything. Stay, stay," added the Jew, unlocking a drawer with a shaking hand; "there's money, my dears. I shall shut up this shop to-night: you'll know where to find me. Don't stop here a minute,—not an instant, my dears!"

With these words he pushed them from the room, and carefully double-locking and barring the door behind them, drew from its place of concealment the box which he had unintentionally disclosed to Oliver, and hastily proceeded to dispose the watches and jewellery beneath his clothing.

A rap at the door startled him in this occupation. "Who's there?" he cried in a shrill tone of alarm.

"Me!" replied the voice of the Dodger through the key-hole.

"What now?" cried the Jew impatiently.

"Is he to be kidnapped to the other ken, Nancy says?" inquired the Dodger cautiously.

"Yes," replied the Jew, "wherever she lays hands on him. Find him, find him out, that's all. I shall know what to do next, never fear."

The boy murmured a reply of intelligence, and hurried down stairs after his companions.

"He has not peached so far," said the Jew as he pursued his occupation. "If he means to blab us among his new friends, we may stop his windpipe yet."

CHAPTER XIV.

COMPRISING FURTHER PARTICULARS OF OLIVER'S STAY AT MR. BROWNLOW'S, WITH THE REMARKABLE PREDICTION WHICH ONE MR. GRIMWIG UTTERED CONCERNING HIM, WHEN HE WENT OUT ON AN ERRAND.

OLIVER soon recovered from the fainting-fit into which Mr. Brownlow's abrupt exclamation had thrown him; and the subject of the picture was carefully avoided, both by the old gentleman and Mrs. Bedwin, in the conversation that ensued, which indeed bore no reference to Oliver's history or prospects, but was confined to such topics as might amuse without exciting him. He was still too weak to get up to breakfast; but, when he came down into the housekeeper's room next day, his first act was to cast an eager glance at the wall, in the hope of again looking on the face of the beautiful lady. His expectations were disappointed, however, for the picture had been removed.

"Ah!" said the housekeeper, watching the direction of Oliver's eyes. "It is gone, you see."

"I see it is, ma'am," replied Oliver, with a sigh. "Why have they taken it away?"

"It has been taken down, child, because Mr. Brownlow said, that, as it seemed to worry you, perhaps it might prevent your getting well, you know," rejoined the old lady.

"Oh, no, indeed it didn't worry me, ma'am," said Oliver. "I liked to see it; I quite loved it."

"Well, well!" said the old lady, good-humouredly; "you get well as fast as ever you can, dear, and it shall be hung up again. There, I promise you that; now let us talk about something else."

This was all the information Oliver could obtain about the picture at that time, and as the old lady had been so kind to him in his illness, he endeavoured to think no more of the subject just then; so listened attentively to a great many stories she told him about an amiable and handsome daughter of hers, who was married to an amiable and handsome man, and lived in the country; and a son, who was clerk to a merchant in the West Indies, and who was also such a good young man, and wrote such dutiful letters home four times a year, that it brought the tears into her eyes to talk about them. When the old lady had expatiated a long time on the excellences of her children, and the merits of her kind good husband besides, who had been dead and gone, poor dear soul! just six-and-twenty years, it was time to have tea; and after tea she began to teach Oliver cribbage, which he learnt as quickly as she could teach, and at which game they played, with great interest and gravity, until it was time for the invalid to have some warm wine and water, with a slice of dry toast, and to go cosily to bed.

They were happy days those of Oliver's recovery. Everything was so quiet, and neat, and orderly: everybody so kind and gentle, that after the noise and turbulence in the midst of which he had always lived, it seemed like heaven itself. He was no sooner strong enough to put his clothes on properly, than Mr. Brownlow caused a complete new suit, and a new cap, and a new pair of shoes, to be provided for him. As Oliver was told that he might do what he liked with the old clothes, he gave them to a servant who had been very kind to him, and asked her to sell them to a Jew, and keep the money for herself. This she very readily did; and, as Oliver looked out of the parlour window, and saw the Jew roll them up in his bag and walk away, he felt quite delighted to think that they were safely gone, and that there was now no possible danger of his ever being able to wear them again. They were sad rags, to tell the truth; and Oliver had never had a new suit before.

One evening, about a week after the affair of the picture, as he was sitting talking to Mrs. Bedwin, there came a message down from Mr. Brownlow, that if Oliver Twist felt pretty well, he should like to see him in his study, and talk to him a little while.

"Bless us, and save us! wash your hands, and let me part your hair nicely for you, child," said Mrs. Bedwin. "Dear heart alive! if we had known he would have asked for you, we would have put you a clean collar on, and made you as smart as sixpence."

Oliver did as the old lady bade him, and, although she lamented grievously meanwhile that there was not even time to crimp the little frill that bordered his shirt-collar, he looked so delicate and handsome, despite that important personal advantage, that she went so far as to say, looking at him with great complacency from head to foot, that she really didn't think it would have been possible on the longest notice to have made much difference in him for the better.

Thus encouraged, Oliver tapped at the study door, and, on Mr. Brownlow calling to him to come in, found himself in a little back room quite full of books, with a window looking into some pleasant little gardens. There was a table drawn up before the window, at which Mr. Brownlow was seated reading. When he saw Oliver, he pushed the book away from him, and told him to come near the table and sit down. Oliver complied, marvelling where the people could be found to read such a great number of books as seemed to be written to make the world wiser,—which is still a marvel to more experienced people than Oliver Twist every day of their lives.

"There are a good many books, are there not, my boy?" said Mr. Brownlow, observing the curiosity with which Oliver surveyed the shelves that reached from the floor to the ceiling.

"A great number, sir," replied Oliver; "I never saw so many."

"You shall read them if you behave well," said the old gentleman kindly; "and you will like that, better than looking at the outsides,— that is, in some cases, because there *are* books of which the backs and covers are by far the best parts."

"I suppose they are those heavy ones, sir," said Oliver, pointing to some large quartos with a good deal of gilding about the binding.

"Not always those," said the old gentleman,

patting Oliver on the head, and smiling as he did so; "there are other equally heavy ones, though of a much smaller size. How should you like to grow up a clever man, and write books, eh?"

"I think I would rather read them, sir," replied Oliver.

"What! wouldn't you like to be a book-writer?" said the old gentleman.

Oliver considered a little while, and at last said he should think it would be a much better thing to be a bookseller; upon which the old gentleman laughed heartily, and declared he had said a very good thing, which Oliver felt glad to have done, though he by no means knew what it was.

"Well, well," said the old gentleman, composing his features, "don't be afraid; we won't make an author of you, while there's an honest trade to be learnt, or brick-making to turn to."

"Thank you, sir," said Oliver; and at the earnest manner of his reply the old gentleman laughed again, and said something about a curious instinct, which Oliver, not understanding, paid no very great attention to.

"Now," said Mr. Brownlow, speaking if possible in a kinder, but at the same time in a much more serious manner than Oliver had ever heard him speak in yet, "I want you to pay great attention, my boy, to what I am going to say. I shall talk to you without any reserve, because I am sure you are as well able to understand me as many older persons would be."

"Oh, don't tell me you are going to send me away, sir, pray!" exclaimed Oliver, alarmed by the serious tone of the old gentleman's commencement! "don't turn me out of doors to wander in the streets again. Let me stay here and be a servant. Don't send me back to the wretched place I came from. Have mercy upon a poor boy, sir; do?"

"My dear child," said the old gentleman, moved by the warmth of Oliver's sudden appeal, "you need not be afraid of my deserting you, unless you give me cause."

"I never, never will, sir," interposed Oliver.

"I hope not," rejoined the old gentleman; "I do not think you ever will. I have been deceived before, in the objects whom I have endeavoured to benefit; but I feel strongly disposed to trust you, nevertheless, and more interested in your behalf than I can well account for, even to myself. The persons on whom I have bestowed my dearest love lie deep in their graves; but, although the happiness and delight of my life lie buried there too, I have not made a coffin of my heart, and sealed it up for ever on my best affections. Deep affliction has only made them stronger; it ought, I think, for it should refine our nature."

As the old gentleman said this in a low voice, more to himself than to his companion, and remained silent for a short time afterwards, Oliver sat quite still, almost afraid to breathe.

"Well, well," said the old gentleman at length in a more cheerful tone, "I only say this, because you have a young heart, and knowing that I have suffered great pain and sorrow, you will be more careful, perhaps, not to wound me again. You say you are an orphan, without a friend in the world; all the inquiries I have been able to make confirm the statement. Let me hear your story; where you came from, who brought you up, and how you got into the company in which I found you. Speak the truth; and if I find you have committed no crime, you will never be friendless while I live."

Oliver's sobs checked his utterance for some minutes; and when he was on the point of beginning to relate how he had been brought up at the farm, and carried to the workhouse by Mr. Bumble, a peculiarly impatient little double-knock was heard at the street-door, and the servant, running up stairs, announced Mr. Grimwig.

"Is he coming up?" inquired Mr. Brownlow.

"Yes, sir," replied the servant. "He asked if there were any muffins in the house, and, when I told him yes, he said he had come to tea."

Mr. Brownlow smiled, and, turning to Oliver, said Mr. Grimwig was an old friend of his, and he must not mind his being a little rough in his manners, for he was a worthy creature at bottom, as he had reason to know.

"Shall I go down stairs, sir?" inquired Oliver.

"No," replied Mr. Brownlow; "I would rather you stopped here."

At this moment there walked into the room, supporting himself by a thick stick, a stout old gentleman, rather lame in one leg, who was dressed in a blue coat, striped waistcoat, nankeen breeches and gaiters, and a broad-brimmed white hat, with the sides turned up with green. A very small-plaited shirt-frill stuck out from his waistcoat, and a very long steel watch-chain, with nothing but a key at the end, dangled loosely below it. The ends of his white neckerchief were twisted into a ball about the size of an orange;—the variety of shapes into which his countenance was twisted defy description. He had a manner of screwing his head round on one side when he spoke, and looking out of the corners of his eyes at the same time, which irresistibly reminded the beholder of a parrot. In this attitude he fixed himself the moment he made his appearance; and, holding out a small piece of orange-peel at arm's length, exclaimed in a growling, discontented voice,

"Look here! do you see this? Isn't it a

most wonderful and extraordinary thing that I can't call at a man's house but I find a piece of this poor-surgeon's-friend on the staircase? I've been lamed with orange-peel once, and I know orange-peel will be my death at last. It will, sir; orange-peel will be my death, or I'll be content to eat my own head, sir!" This was the handsome offer with which Mr. Grimwig backed and confirmed nearly every assertion he made: and it was the more singular in his case, because, even admitting, for the sake of argument, the possibility of scientific improvements being ever brought to that pass which will enable a gentleman to eat his own head in the event of his being so disposed, Mr. Grimwig's head was such a particularly large one, that the most sanguine man alive could hardly entertain a hope of being able to get through it at a sitting—to put entirely out of the question a very thick coating of powder.

"I'll eat my head, sir," repeated Mr. Grimwig, striking his stick upon the ground. "Hallo! what's that?" he added, looking at Oliver, and retreating a pace or two.

"This is young Oliver Twist, whom we were speaking about," said Mr. Brownlow.

Oliver bowed.

"You don't mean to say that's the boy that had the fever, I hope?" said Mr. Grimwig, recoiling a little further. "Wait a minute, don't speak: stop—" continued Mr. Grimwig abruptly, losing all dread of the fever in his triumph at the discovery; "that's the boy that had the orange! If that's not the boy, sir, that had the orange, and threw this bit of peel upon the staircase, I'll eat my head and his too."

"No, no, he has not had one," said Mr. Brownlow, laughing. "Come, put down your hat, and speak to my young friend."

"I feel strongly on this subject, sir," said the irritable old gentleman, drawing off his gloves. "There's always more or less orange-peel on the pavement in our street, and I *know* it's put there by the surgeon's boy at the corner. A young woman stumbled over a bit last night, and fell against my garden-railings; directly she got up I saw her look towards his infernal red lamp with the pantomime-light. 'Don't go to him,' I called out of the window, 'he's an assassin,—a man-trap!' So he is. If he is not——" Here the irascible old gentleman gave a great knock on the ground with his stick, which was always understood by his friends to imply the customary offer whenever it was not expressed in words. Then, still keeping his stick in his hand, he sat down, and, opening a double eye-glass which he wore attached to a broad black riband, took a view of Oliver, who, seeing that he was the object of inspection, coloured, and bowed again.

"That's the boy, is it?" said Mr. Grimwig, at length.

"That is the boy," replied Mr. Brownlow, nodding good-humouredly to Oliver.

"How are you, boy?" said Mr. Grimwig.

"A great deal better, thank you, sir," replied Oliver.

Mr. Brownlow, seeming to apprehend that his singular friend was about to say something disagreeable, asked Oliver to step down stairs and tell Mrs. Bedwin they were ready for tea, which, as he did not half like the visitor's manner, he was very happy to do.

"He is a nice-looking boy, is he not?" inquired Mr. Brownlow.

"I don't know," replied Grimwig, pettishly.

"Don't know?"

"No, I don't know. I never see any difference in boys. I only know two sorts of boys,—mealy boys, and beef-faced boys."

"And which is Oliver!"

"Mealy. I know a friend who's got a beef-faced boy; a fine boy they call him, with a round head, and red cheeks, and glaring eyes; a horrid boy, with a body and limbs that appear to be swelling out of the seams of his blue clothes—with the voice of a pilot, and the appetite of a wolf. I know him, the wretch!"

"Come," said Mr. Brownlow, "these are not the characteristics of young Oliver Twist; so he needn't excite your wrath."

"They are not," replied Grimwig. "He may have worse."

Here Mr. Brownlow coughed impatiently,

which appeared to afford Mr. Grimwig the most exquisite delight.

"He may have worse, I say," repeated Mr. Grimwig. "Where does he come from? Who is he? What is he? He has had a fever—what of that? Fevers are not peculiar to good people, are they? Bad people have fevers sometimes, haven't they, eh? I knew a man that was hung in Jamaica for murdering his master; he had had a fever six times; he wasn't recommended to mercy on that account. Pooh! nonsense!"

Now, the fact was, that, in the inmost recesses of his own heart, Mr. Grimwig was strongly disposed to admit that Oliver's appearance and manner were unusually prepossessing, but he had a strong appetite for contradiction, sharpened on this occasion by the finding of the orange-peel; and inwardly determining that no man should dictate to him whether a boy was well-looking or not, he had resolved from the first to oppose his friend. When Mr. Brownlow admitted that on no one point of inquiry could he yet return a satisfactory answer, and that he had postponed any investigation into Oliver's previous history until he thought the boy was strong enough to bear it, Mr. Grimwig chuckled maliciously, and demanded, with a sneer, whether the housekeeper was in the habit of counting the plate at night; because, if she didn't find a table-spoon or two missing some sunshiny morning, why, he would be content to——, et cetera.

All this, Mr. Brownlow, although himself somewhat of an impetuous gentleman, knowing his friend's peculiarities, bore with great good humour; as Mr. Grimwig, at tea, was graciously pleased to express his entire approval of the muffins, matters went on very smoothly; and Oliver, who made one of the party, began to feel more at his ease than he had yet done in the fierce old gentleman's presence.

"And when are you going to hear a full, true, and particular account of the life and adventures of Oliver Twist?" asked Grimwig of Mr. Brownlow, at the conclusion of the meal: looking sideways at Oliver as he resumed the subject.

"To-morrow morning," replied Mr. Brownlow. "I would rather he was alone with me at the time. Come up to me to-morrow morning at ten o'clock, my dear."

"Yes, sir," replied Oliver. He answered with some hesitation, because he was confused by Mr. Grimwig's looking so hard at him.

"I'll tell you what," whispered that gentleman to Mr. Brownlow; "he won't come up to you to-morrow morning. I saw him hesitate. He is deceiving you, my dear friend."

"I'll swear he is not," replied Mr. Brownlow, warmly.

"If he is not," said Mr. Grimwig, "I'll ———" and down went the stick.

"I'll answer for that boy's truth with my life," said Mr. Brownlow, knocking the table.

"And I for his falsehood with my head," rejoined Mr. Grimwig, knocking the table also.

"We shall see," said Mr. Brownlow, checking his rising passion.

"We will," replied Mr. Grimwig, with a provoking smile; "we will."

As fate would have it, Mrs. Bedwin chanced

to bring in at this moment a small parcel of books which Mr. Brownlow had that morning purchased of the identical bookstall-keeper who has already figured in this history; which having laid on the table, she prepared to leave the room.

"Stop the boy, Mrs. Bedwin," said Mr. Brownlow; "there is something to go back."

"He has gone, sir," replied Mrs. Bedwin.

"Call after him," said Mr. Brownlow; "it's particular. He is a poor man, and they are not paid for. There are some books to be taken back, too."

The street-door was opened. Oliver ran one way, and the girl another, and Mrs. Bedwin stood on the step and screamed for the boy; but there was no boy in sight, and both Oliver and the girl returned in a breathless state to report that there were no tidings of him.

"Dear me, I am very sorry for that," exclaimed Mr. Brownlow; "I particularly wished those books to be returned to-night."

"Send Oliver with them," said Mr. Grimwig

with an ironical smile; "he will be sure to deliver them safely, you know."

"Yes; do let me take them, if you please, sir," said Oliver; "I'll run all the way, sir."

The old gentleman was just going to say that Oliver should not go out on any account, when a most malicious cough from Mr. Grimwig determined him that he should, and by his prompt discharge of the commission prove to him the injustice of his suspicions, on this head at least, at once.

"You *shall* go, my dear," said the old gentleman. "The books are on a chair by my table. Fetch them down."

Oliver, delighted to be of use, brought down the books under his arm in a great bustle, and waited, cap in hand, to hear what message he was to take.

"You are to say," said Mr. Brownlow, glancing steadily at Grimwig,—"you are to say that you have brought those books back, and that you have come to pay the four pound ten I owe him. This is a five-pound note, so you will have to bring me back ten shillings change."

" I won't be ten minutes, sir," replied Oliver, eagerly; and, having buttoned up the bank-note in his jacket pocket, and placed the books carefully under his arm, he made a respectful bow, and left the room. Mrs. Bedwin followed him to the street-door, giving him many directions about the nearest way, and the name of the bookseller, and the name of the street, all of which Oliver said he clearly understood; and, having superadded many injunctions to be sure and not take cold, the careful old lady at length permitted him to depart.

"Bless his sweet face!" said the old lady, looking after him. "I can't bear, somehow, to let him go out of my sight."

At this moment, Oliver looked gaily round, and nodded before he turned the corner. The old lady smilingly returned his salutation, and, closing the door, went back to her own room.

"Let me see; he'll be back in twenty minutes, at the longest," said Mr. Brownlow, pulling out his watch, and placing it on the table. " It will be dark by that time."

" Oh! you really expect him to come back, do you?" inquired Mr. Grimwig.

" Don't you?" asked Mr. Brownlow, smiling.

The spirit of contradiction was strong in Mr. Grimwig's breast at the moment, and it was rendered stronger by his friend's confident smile.

" No," he said, smiting the table with his fist, " I do not. The boy has a new suit of clothes on his back, a set of valuable books under his arm, and a five-pound note in his pocket; he'll join his old friends the thieves, and laugh at you. If ever that boy returns to this house, sir, I'll eat my head."

With these words he drew his chair closer to the table, and there the two friends sat in silent expectation, with the watch between them. It is worthy of remark, as illustrating the importance we attach to our own judgments, and the pride with which we put forth our most rash and hasty conclusions, that, although Mr. Grimwig was not by any means a bad-hearted man, and would have been unfeignedly sorry to see his respected friend duped and deceived, he really did most earnestly and strongly hope at that moment that Oliver Twist might not come back. Of such contradictions is human nature made up!

It grew so dark that the figures on the dial were scarcely discernible; but there the two old gentlemen continued to sit in silence, with the watch between them.

CHAPTER XV.

SHOWING HOW VERY FOND OF OLIVER TWIST, THE MERRY OLD JEW AND MISS NANCY WERE.

In the obscure parlour of a low public-house, situate in the filthiest part of Little Saffron-Hill, —a dark and gloomy den, where a flaring gas-light burnt all day in the winter-time, and where no ray of sun ever shone in the summer,—there sat, brooding over a little pewter measure and a small glass, strongly impregnated with the smell of liquor, a man in a velveteen coat, drab shorts, half-boots, and stockings, whom, even by that dim light, no experienced agent of police would have hesitated for one instant to recognise as Mr. William Sikes. At his feet sat a white-coated, red-eyed dog, who occupied himself alternately in winking at his master with both eyes at the same time, and in licking a large, fresh cut on one side of his mouth, which appeared to be the result of some recent conflict.

"Keep quiet, you warmint! keep quiet!" said Mr. Sikes, suddenly breaking silence. Whether his meditations were so intense as to be disturbed by the dog's winking, or whether his feelings were so wrought upon by his reflections that they required all the relief derivable from kicking an unoffending animal to allay them, is matter for argument and consideration. Whatever was the cause, the effect was a kick and a curse bestowed upon the dog simultaneously.

Dogs are not generally apt to revenge injuries inflicted upon them by their masters; but Mr. Sikes's dog, having faults of temper in common with his owner, and labouring perhaps, at this moment, under a powerful sense of injury, made no more ado but at once fixed his teeth in one of the half-boots, and, having given it a good hearty shake, retired, growling, under a form; thereby just escaping the pewter measure which Mr. Sikes levelled at his head.

"You would, would you?" said Sikes, seizing the poker in one hand, and deliberately opening with the other a large clasp-knife, which he drew from his pocket. "Come here, you born devil! Come here! D'ye hear?"

The dog no doubt heard, because Mr. Sikes spoke in the very harshest key of a very harsh voice; but, appearing to entertain some unaccountable objection to having his throat cut, he remained where he was, and growled more fiercely than before, at the same time grasping the end of the poker between his teeth, and biting at it like a wild beast.

This resistance only infuriated Mr. Sikes the more; who, dropping on his knees, began to assail the animal most furiously. The dog jumped from right to left, and from left to right, snapping, growling, and barking; the man thrust and swore, and struck and blasphemed; and the struggle was reaching a most critical point for one or other, when, the door suddenly opening, the dog darted out, leaving Bill Sikes with the poker and the clasp-knife in his hands.

There must always be two parties to a quarrel, says the old adage. Mr. Sikes, being disappointed of the dog's presence, at once transferred the quarrel to the new-comer.

"What the devil do you come in between me and my dog for?" said Sikes with a fierce gesture.

"I didn't know, my dear, I didn't know," replied Fagin humbly—for the Jew was the new-comer.

"Didn't know, you white-livered thief!" growled Sikes. "Couldn't you hear the noise?"

"Not a sound of it, as I'm a living man, Bill," replied the Jew.

"Oh no, you hear nothing, you don't," retorted Sikes with a fierce sneer, " sneaking in and out, so as nobody hears how you come or go. I wish you had been the dog, Fagin, half a minute ago."

"Why?" inquired the Jew with a forced smile.

"'Cause the government, as cares for the lives of such men as you, as haven't half the pluck of curs, lets a man kill his dog how he likes," replied Sikes, shutting up the knife with a very expressive look; "that's why."

The Jew rubbed his hands, and, sitting down at the table, affected to laugh at the pleasantry of his friend,—obviously very ill at his ease, however.

"Grin away," said Sikes, replacing the poker, and surveying him with savage contempt; "grin away. You'll never have the laugh at me, though, unless it's behind a nightcap. I've got the upper hand over you, Fagin; and, d—— me, I'll keep it. There. If I go, you go; so take care of me."

"Well, well, my dear," said the Jew, "I know all that; we—we—have a mutual interest, Bill,—a mutual interest."

"Humph," said Sikes, as if he thought the interest lay rather more on the Jew's side than on his. "Well, what have you got to say to me?"

"It's all passed safe through the melting-pot," replied Fagin, "and this is your share. It's rather more than it ought to be, my dear; but as I know you'll do me a good turn another time, and——"

"'Stow that gammon," interposed the robber impatiently. "Where is it? Hand over!"

"Yes, yes, Bill; give me time, give me time," replied the Jew soothingly. "Here it is—all safe." As he spoke, he drew forth an old cotton handkerchief from his breast, and untying a large knot in one corner, produced a small brown-paper packet, which Sikes snatching from him, hastily opened, and proceeded to count the sovereigns it contained.

"This is all, is it?" inquired Sikes.

"All," replied the Jew.

"You haven't opened the parcel and swallowed one or two as you come along, have you?" inquired Sikes suspiciously. "Don't put on a injured look at the question; you've done it many a time. Jerk the tinkler."

These words, in plain English, conveyed an injunction to ring the bell. It was answered by another Jew, younger than Fagin, but nearly as vile and repulsive in appearance.

Bill Sikes merely pointed to the empty measure, and the Jew, perfectly understanding the hint, retired to fill it, previously exchanging a remarkable look with Fagin, who raised his eyes for an instant, as if in expectation of it, and shook his head in reply so slightly that the action would have been almost imperceptible to a third person. It was lost upon Sikes, who was stooping at the moment to tie the boot-lace which the dog had torn. Possibly if he had observed the brief interchange of signals, he might have thought that it boded no good to him.

"Is anybody here, Barney?" inquired Fagin, speaking—now that Sikes was looking on—without raising his eyes from the ground.

"Dot a shoul," replied Barney, whose words, whether they came from the heart or not, made their way through the nose.

"Nobody?" inquired Fagin in a tone of surprise, which perhaps might mean that Barney was at liberty to tell the truth.

"Dobody but Biss Dadsy," replied Barney.

"Nancy!" exclaimed Sikes. "Where? Strike me blind, if I don't honor that 'ere girl for her native talents."

"She's bid havid a plate of boiled beef id the bar," replied Barney.

"Send her here," said Sikes, pouring out a glass of liquor. "Send her here."

Barney looked timidly at Fagin, as if for permission; the Jew remaining silent, and not lifting his eyes from the ground, he retired, and presently returned ushering in Nancy, who was decorated with the bonnet, apron, basket, and street-door key complete.

"You are on the scent, are you, Nancy?" inquired Sikes, proffering the glass.

"Yes, I am, Bill," replied the young lady, disposing of its contents; "and tired enough of it I am, too. The young brat's been ill and confined to the crib; and——"

"Ah, Nancy, dear!" said Fagin, looking up.

Now, whether a peculiar contraction of the Jew's red eye-brows, and a half-closing of his deeply-set eyes, warned Miss Nancy that she was disposed to be too communicative, is not a matter of much importance. The fact is all we need care for here; and the fact is, that she suddenly checked herself, and with several gracious smiles upon Mr. Sikes, turned the conversation to other matters. In about ten minutes' time, Mr. Fagin was seized with a fit of coughing, upon which Nancy pulled her shawl over her shoulders, and declared it was time to go. Mr. Sikes, finding that he was walking a short part of her way himself, expressed his intention of accompanying her, and they went away together, followed at a little distance by the dog, who slunk out of a back-yard as soon as his master was out of sight.

The Jew thrust his head out of the room door when Sikes had left it, looked after him as he walked up the dark passage, shook his clenched fist, muttered a deep curse, and then with a horrible grin re-seated himself at the table, where he was soon deeply absorbed in the interesting pages of the Hue-and-Cry.

Meanwhile Oliver Twist, little dreaming that he was within so very short a distance of the merry old gentleman, was on his way to the bookstall. When he got into Clerkenwell he accidentally turned down a by-street which was not exactly in his way; but not discovering his mistake till he had got halfway down it, and knowing it must lead in the right direction, he did not think it worth while to turn back, and so marched on as quickly as he could, with the books under his arm.

He was walking along, thinking how happy and contented he ought to feel, and how much he would give for only one look at poor little Dick, who, starved and beaten, might be weeping bitterly at that very moment, when he was startled by a young woman screaming out very loud, " Oh, my dear brother!" and he had hardly looked up to see what the matter was, when he was stopped by having a pair of arms thrown tight round his neck.

" Don't!" cried Oliver, struggling. " Let go of me. Who is it? What are you stopping me for?"

The only reply to this, was a great number of loud lamentations from the young woman who had embraced him, and who had a little basket and a street-door key in her hand.

" Oh my gracious!" said the young woman, " I've found him! Oh, Oliver! Oliver! Oh, you naughty boy, to make me suffer such distress on your account! Come home, dear, come. Oh, I've found him. Thank gracious goodness heavins, I 've found him!" With these incoherent exclamations the young woman burst into another fit of crying, and got so dreadfully hysterical, that a couple of women who came up at the moment asked a butcher's boy with a shiny head of hair anointed with suet, who was also looking on, whether he didn't think he had better run for the doctor. To which the butcher's boy, who appeared of a lounging, not to say indolent disposition, replied that he thought not.

"Oh, no, no, never mind," said the young woman, grasping Oliver's hand; "I 'm better now. Come home directly, you cruel boy. Come."

"What's the matter, ma'am?" inquired one of the women.

"Oh, ma'am," replied the young woman, "he ran away near a month ago from his parents, who are hard-working and respectable people, and joined a set of thieves and bad characters, and almost broke his mother's heart."

"Young wretch!" said one woman.

"Go home, do, you little brute," said the other.

"I'm not," replied Oliver, greatly alarmed. "I don't know her. I haven't any sister, or father and mother either. I'm an orphan; I live at Pentonville."

"Oh, only hear him, how he braves it out!" cried the young woman.

"Why, it's Nancy!" exclaimed Oliver, who now saw her face for the first time, and started back in irrepressible astonishment.

"You see he knows me," cried Nancy, appealing to the by-standers. "He can't help himself. Make him come home, there's good people, or he'll kill his dear mother and father, and break my heart!"

"What the devil's this?" said a man, bursting out of a beer-shop, with a white dog at his heels; "young Oliver! Come home to your poor mother, you young dog! come home directly."

"I don't belong to them. I don't know them. Help! help!" cried Oliver, struggling in the man's powerful grasp.

"Help!" repeated the man. "Yes; I'll help you, you young rascal! What books are these? You've been a-stealing 'em, have you? Give 'em here!" With these words the man tore the volumes from his grasp, and struck him violently on the head.

"That's right!" cried a looker-on, from a garret-window. "That's the only way of bringing him to his senses!"

"To be sure," cried a sleepy-faced carpenter, casting an approving look at the garret-window.

"It'll do him good!" said the two women.

"And he shall have it, too!" rejoined the man, administering another blow, and seizing Oliver by the collar. "Come on, you young villain! Here, Bull's-eye, mind him, boy! mind him!"

Weak with recent illness, stupified by the blows and the suddenness of the attack, terrified by the fierce growling of the dog and the brutality of the man, and overpowered by the conviction of the by-standers that he was really the hardened little wretch he was described to be, what could one poor child do! Darkness had set in; it was a low neighbourhood; no help

was near; resistance was useless. In another moment he was dragged into a labyrinth of dark narrow courts, and forced along them at a pace which rendered the few cries he dared to give utterance to, wholly unintelligible. It was of little moment, indeed, whether they were intelligible or not, for there was nobody to care for them had they been ever so plain.

* * * * *

The gas-lamps were lighted; Mrs. Bedwin was waiting anxiously at the open door; the servant had run up the street twenty times to see if there were any traces of Oliver; and still the two old gentlemen sat perseveringly in the dark parlour, with the watch between them.

CHAPTER XVI.

RELATES WHAT BECAME OF OLIVER TWIST, AFTER HE HAD BEEN CLAIMED BY NANCY.

The narrow streets and courts at length terminated in a large open space, scattered about which, were pens for beasts, and other indications of a cattle-market. Sikes slackened his pace when they reached this spot, the girl being quite unable to support any longer the rapid rate at which they had hitherto walked. Turning to Oliver, he roughly commanded him to take hold of Nancy's hand.

"Do you hear?" growled Sikes, as Oliver hesitated, and looked round.

They were in a dark corner, quite out of the track of passengers, and Oliver saw but too plainly that resistance would be of no avail.

He held out his hand, which Nancy clasped tight in hers.

"Give me the other," said Sikes, seizing Oliver's unoccupied hand. "Here, Bull's-eye!"

The dog looked up, and growled.

"See here, boy!" said Sikes, putting his other hand to Oliver's throat, and uttering a savage oath; "if he speaks ever so soft a word, hold him! D'ye mind?"

The dog growled again, and, licking his lips, eyed Oliver as if he were anxious to attach himself to his windpipe without any unnecessary delay.

"He's as willing as a Christian, strike me blind if he isn't!" said Sikes, regarding the animal with a kind of grim and ferocious approval.

"Now, you know what you've got to expect, master, so call away as quick as you like; the dog will soon stop that game. Get on, young 'un!"

Bull's-eye wagged his tail in acknowledgment of this unusually endearing form of speech, and, giving vent to another admonitory growl for the benefit of Oliver, led the way onward.

It was Smithfield that they were crossing, although it might have been Grosvenor Square, for anything Oliver knew to the contrary. The night was dark and foggy. The lights in the shops could scarcely struggle through the heavy mist, which thickened every moment and shrouded the streets and houses in gloom, rendering the strange place still stranger in Oliver's eyes, and making his uncertainty the more dismal and depressing.

They had hurried on a few paces, when a deep church-bell struck the hour. With its first stroke his two conductors stopped, and turned their heads in the direction whence the sound proceeded.

"Eight o'clock, Bill," said Nancy, when the bell ceased.

"What's the good of telling me that; I can hear it, can't I?" replied Sikes.

"I wonder whether *they* can hear it," said Nancy.

"Of course they can," replied Sikes. "It was Bartlemy time when I was shopped, and there warn't a penny trumpet in the fair as I couldn't hear the squeaking on. Arter I was locked up for the night, the row and din outside made the thundering old jail so silent, that I could almost have beat my head out against the iron plates of the door."

" Poor fellows!" said Nancy, who still had her face turned towards the quarter in which the bell had sounded. " Oh, Bill, such fine young chaps as them!"

" Yes; that's all you women think of," answered Sikes. " Fine young chaps! Well, they're as good as dead, so it don't much matter."

With this consolation Mr. Sikes appeared to repress a rising tendency to jealousy, and, clasping Oliver's wrist more firmly, told him to step out again.

" Wait a minute," said the girl: " I wouldn't hurry by, if it was you that was coming out to be hung the next time eight o'clock struck, Bill. I'd walk round and round the place till I dropped, if the snow was on the ground, and I hadn't a shawl to cover me."

" And what good would that do?" inquired

the unsentimental Mr. Sikes. " Unless you could pitch over a file and twenty yards of good stout rope, you might as well be walking fifty mile off, or not walking at all, for all the good it would do me. Come on, will you, and don't stand preaching there."

The girl burst into a laugh, drew her shawl more closely round her, and they walked away. But Oliver felt her hand tremble; and, looking up in her face as they passed a gas-lamp, saw that it had turned a deadly white.

They walked on, by little-frequented and dirty ways, for a full half-hour, meeting very few people, and those they did meet, appearing from their looks to hold much the same position in society as Mr. Sikes himself. At length they turned into a very filthy narrow street, nearly full of old-clothes shops; the dog, running forward as if conscious that there was no further occasion for his keeping on guard, stopped before the door of a shop which was closed and apparently untenanted, for the house was in a ruinous condition, and upon the door was nailed a board intimating that it was to let, which looked as if it had hung there for many years.

"All right," said Sikes, glancing cautiously about.

Nancy stooped below the shutters, and Oliver heard the sound of a bell. They crossed to the opposite side of the street, and stood for a few moments under a lamp. A noise, as if a sash-window were gently raised, was heard, and soon afterwards the door softly opened; upon which Mr. Sikes seized the terrified boy by the collar with very little ceremony, and all three were quickly inside the house.

The passage was perfectly dark, and they waited while the person who had let them in chained and barred the door.

"Anybody here?" inquired Sikes.

"No," replied a voice, which Oliver thought he had heard before.

"Is the old 'un here?" asked the robber.

"Yes," replied the voice; "and precious down in the mouth he has been. Won't he be glad to see you? Oh, no!"

The style of this reply, as well as the voice

which delivered it, seemed familiar to Oliver's ears; but it was impossible to distinguish even the form of the speaker in the darkness.

"Let's have a glim," said Sikes, "or we shall go breaking our necks, or treading on the dog. Look after your legs if you do, that's all."

"Stand still a moment, and I'll get you one," replied the voice. The receding footsteps of the speaker were heard, and in another minute the form of Mr. John Dawkins, otherwise the artful Dodger, appeared, bearing in his right hand a tallow candle stuck in the end of a cleft stick.

The young gentleman did not stop to bestow any other mark of recognition upon Oliver than a humorous grin; but, turning away, beckoned the visiters to follow him down a flight of stairs. They crossed an empty kitchen, and, opening the door of a low earthy-smelling room, which seemed to have been built in a small back-yard were received with a shout of laughter.

"Oh, my wig, my wig!" cried Master Charles Bates, from whose lungs the laughter had proceeded; "here he is!—oh, cry, here he is! Oh, Fagin, look at him; Fagin, do look at him! I can't bear it; it is such a jolly game, I can't bear it. Hold me, somebody, while I laugh it out."

With this irrepressible ebullition of mirth, Master Bates laid himself flat on the floor, and kicked convulsively for five minutes in an ecstasy of facetious joy. Then, jumping to his feet, he snatched the cleft stick from the Dodger, and, advancing to Oliver, viewed him round and round, while the Jew, taking off his nightcap, made a great number of low bows to the bewildered boy; the Artful meantime, who was of a rather saturnine disposition, and seldom gave way to merriment when it interfered with business, rifling his pockets with steady assiduity.

"Look at his togs, Fagin!" said Charley, putting the light so close to Oliver's new jacket as nearly to set him on fire. "Look at his togs!—superfine cloth, and the heavy-swell cut! Oh, my eye, what a game! And his books, too;—nothing but a gentleman, Fagin!"

"Delighted to see you looking so well, my dear," said the Jew, bowing with mock humility. "The Artful shall give you another suit, my dear, for fear you should spoil that Sunday one. Why didn't you write, my dear, and say you were coming?—we'd have got something warm for supper."

At this, Master Bates roared again: so loud that Fagin himself relaxed, and even the Dodger smiled; but as the Artful drew forth the five-pound note at that instant, it is doubtful whether the sally or the discovery awakened his merriment.

"Hallo! what's that?" inquired Sikes, stepping forward as the Jew seized the note. "That's mine, Fagin."

"No, no, my dear," said the Jew. "Mine, Bill, mine. You shall have the books."

"If that ain't mine!" said Sikes, putting on his hat with a determined air,—"mine and Nancy's, that is,—I'll take the boy back again."

The Jew started, and Oliver started too, though from a very different cause, for he hoped that the dispute might really end in his being taken back.

"Come, hand over, will you?" said Sikes.

"This is hardly fair, Bill; hardly fair, is it, Nancy?" inquired the Jew.

"Fair, or not fair," retorted Sikes, "hand it over, I tell you! Do you think Nancy and me has got nothing else to do with our precious time but to spend it in scouting arter and kidnapping every young boy as gets grabbed through you? Give it here, you avaricious old skeleton; give it here!"

With this gentle remonstrance, Mr. Sikes plucked the note from between the Jew's finger and thumb; and, looking the old man coolly in the face, folded it up small, and tied it in his neckerchief.

"That's for our share of the trouble," said Sikes; "and not half enough, neither. You may keep the books, if you're fond of reading, and if not, you can sell 'em."

"They're very pretty," said Charley Bates, who with sundry grimaces had been affecting to read one of the volumes in question; "beautiful writing, isn't it, Oliver?" and at sight of the dismayed look with which Oliver regarded his tormentors, Master Bates, who was blessed with a lively sense of the ludicrous, fell into another ecstasy more boisterous than the first.

"They belong to the old gentleman," said Oliver, wringing his hands,—" to the good kind old gentleman who took me into his house, and had me nursed when I was near dying of the fever. Oh, pray send them back; send him back the books and money. Keep me here all my life long; but pray, pray send them back. He'll think I stole them;—the old lady, all of them that were so kind to me, will think I stole them. Oh, do have mercy upon me, and send them back!"

With these words, which were uttered with all the energy of passionate grief, Oliver fell upon his knees at the Jew's feet, and beat his hands together in perfect desperation.

"The boy's right," remarked Fagin, looking covertly round, and knitting his shaggy eyebrows into a hard knot. "You're right, Oliver, you're right; they *will* think you have stolen 'em. Ha! ha!" chuckled the Jew, rubbing his hands; "it couldn't have happened better if we had chosen our time!"

"Of course it couldn't," replied Sikes; "I know'd that, directly I see him coming through Clerkenwell with the books under his arm. It's all right enough. They're soft-hearted psalm-singers, or they wouldn't have taken him in at all, and they'll ask no questions arter him, fear they should be obliged to prosecute, and so get him lagged. He's safe enough."

Oliver had looked from one to the other while these words were being spoken, as if he were bewildered, and could scarcely understand what passed; but when Bill Sikes concluded, he jumped suddenly to his feet, and tore wildly from the room, uttering shrieks for help which made the bare old house echo to the roof.

"Keep back the dog, Bill!" cried Nancy, springing before the door, and closing it as the Jew and his two pupils darted out in pursuit; "keep back the dog; he'll tear the boy to pieces."

"Serve him right!" cried Sikes, struggling

to disengage himself from the girl's grasp. "Stand off from me, or I'll split your skull against the wall."

"I don't care for that, Bill; I don't care for that," screamed the girl, struggling violently with the man: "the child shan't be torn down by the dog, unless you kill me first."

"Shan't he!" said Sikes, setting his teeth fiercely. "I'll soon do that, if you don't keep off."

The housebreaker flung the girl from him to the further end of the room, just as the Jew and the two boys returned, dragging Oliver among them.

"What's the matter here?" said the Jew, looking round.

"The girl's gone mad, I think," replied Sikes savagely.

"No, she hasn't," said Nancy, pale and breathless from the scuffle; "no, she hasn't, Fagin: don't think it."

"Then keep quiet, will you?" said the Jew with a threatening look.

"No, I won't do that neither," replied Nancy,

speaking very loud. "Come, what do you think of that?"

Mr. Fagin was sufficiently well acquainted with the manners and customs of that particular species of humanity to which Nancy belonged, to feel tolerably certain that it would be rather unsafe to prolong any conversation with her at present. With the view of diverting the attention of the company, he turned to Oliver.

"So you wanted to get away, my dear, did you?" said the Jew, taking up a jagged and knotted club which lay in a corner of the fireplace; "eh?"

Oliver made no reply, but he watched the Jew's motions and breathed quickly.

"Wanted to get assistance,—called for the police, did you?" sneered the Jew, catching the boy by the arm. "We'll cure you of that, my young master."

The Jew inflicted a smart blow on Oliver's shoulders with the club, and was raising it for a second, when the girl, rushing forward, wrested it from his hand, and flung it into the fire with a force that brought some of the glowing coals whirling out into the room.

"I won't stand by and see it done, Fagin," cried the girl. "You've got the boy, and what more would you have? Let him be—let him be, or I shall put that mark on some of you, that will bring me to the gallows before my time."

The girl stamped her foot violently on the floor as she vented this threat; and with her lips compressed, and her hands clenched, looked alternately at the Jew and the other robber—her face quite colourless from the passion of rage into which she had gradually worked herself.

"Why, Nancy!" said the Jew in a soothing tone, after a pause, during which he and Mr. Sikes had stared at one another in a disconcerted manner, "you—you're more clever than ever to-night. Ha! ha! my dear, you are acting beautifully."

"Am I?" said the girl. "Take care I don't overdo it: you will be the worse for it, Fagin, if I do; and so I tell you in good time to keep clear of me."

There is something about a roused woman,

especially if she add to all her other strong passions the fierce impulses of recklessness and despair, which few men like to provoke. The Jew saw that it would be hopeless to affect any further mistake regarding the reality of Miss Nancy's rage; and, shrinking involuntarily back a few paces, cast a glance, half-imploring and half-cowardly, at Sikes, as if to hint that he was the fittest person to pursue the dialogue.

Mr. Sikes thus mutely appealed to, and possibly feeling his personal pride and influence interested in the immediate reduction of Miss Nancy to reason, gave utterance to about a couple of score of curses and threats, the rapid production of which reflected great credit on the fertility of his invention. As they produced no visible effect on the object against whom they were discharged, however, he resorted to more tangible arguments.

"What do you mean by this?" said Sikes, backing the inquiry with a very common imprecation concerning the most beautiful of human features, which, if it were heard above, only once out of every fifty thousand times it is uttered below, would render blindness as common a disorder as measles; "what do you mean by it? Burn my body!—do you know who you are, and what you are?"

"Oh, yes, I know all about it," replied the girl, laughing hysterically, and shaking her head from side to side with a poor assumption of indifference.

"Well, then, keep quiet," rejoined Sikes with a growl like that he was accustomed to use when addressing his dog, "or I'll quiet you for a good long time to come."

The girl laughed again, even less composedly than before, and, darting a hasty look at Sikes, turned her face aside, and bit her lip till the blood came.

"You're a nice one," added Sikes, as he surveyed her with a contemptuous air, "to take up the humane and genteel side! A pretty subject for the child, as you call him, to make a friend of!"

"God Almighty help me, I am!" cried the girl passionately; "and I wish I had been struck dead in the street, or changed places with them we passed so near to-night, before I had lent a hand in bringing him here. He's a thief, a liar, a devil, all that's bad from this night forth. Isn't that enough for the old wretch without blows?"

"Come, come, Sikes," said the Jew, appealing to him in a remonstratory tone, and motioning towards the boys, who were eagerly attentive to all that passed; "we must have civil words,—civil words, Bill."

"Civil words!" cried the girl, whose passion was frightful to see. "Civil words, you villain! Yes; you deserve 'em from me. I thieved for you when I was a child not half as old as this (pointing to Oliver). I have been in the same trade, and in the same service, for twelve years since. Don't you know it? Speak out!—don't you know it?"

"Well, well," replied the Jew, with an attempt at pacification; "and, if you have, it's your living!"

"Ay, it is!" returned the girl: not speaking, but pouring out the words in one continuous and vehement scream. "It is my living, and the cold, wet, dirty streets are my home; and you're the wretch that drove me to them long ago, and that'll keep me there day and night, day and night, till I die!"

"I shall do you a mischief!" interposed the Jew, goaded by these reproaches; "a mischief worse than that, if you say much more!"

The girl said nothing more; but, tearing her hair and dress in a transport of phrensy, made such a rush at the Jew as would probably have left signal marks of her revenge upon him, had not her wrists been seized by Sikes at the right moment; upon which she made a few ineffectual struggles, and fainted.

"She's all right now," said Sikes, laying her down in a corner. "She's uncommon strong in the arms when she's up in this way."

The Jew wiped his forehead, and smiled, as if it were a relief to have the disturbance over; but neither he, nor Sikes, nor the dog, nor the boys, seemed to consider it in any other light than a common occurrence incidental to business.

"It's the worst of having to do with women," said the Jew, replacing the club; "but they're clever, and we can't get on in our line without 'em.—Charley, show Oliver to bed."

"I suppose he'd better not wear his best clothes to-morrow, Fagin, had he?" inquired Charley Bates.

"Certainly not," replied the Jew, reciprocating the grin with which Charley put the question.

Master Bates, apparently much delighted with his commission, took the cleft stick, and led Oliver into an adjacent kitchen, where there were two or three of the beds on which he had slept before; and here, with many uncontrollable bursts of laughter, he produced the identical old suit of clothes which Oliver had so much congratulated himself upon leaving off at Mr. Brownlow's, and the accidental display of which to Fagin by the Jew who purchased them, had been the very first clue received of his whereabout.

"Pull off the smart ones," said Charley, "and I'll give 'em to Fagin to take care of. What fun it is!"

Poor Oliver unwillingly complied; and Master Bates, rolling up the new clothes under his arm, departed from the room, leaving Oliver in the dark, and locking the door behind him.

The noise of Charley's laughter, and the voice of Miss Betsy, who opportunely arrived to throw water over her friend, and perform other feminine offices for the promotion of her recovery, might have kept many people awake under more happy circumstances than those in which Oliver was placed; but he was sick and weary, and soon fell sound asleep.

CHAPTER XVII.

OLIVER'S DESTINY CONTINUING UNPROPITIOUS, BRINGS A GREAT MAN TO LONDON TO INJURE HIS REPUTATION.

It is the custom on the stage in all good, murderous melodramas, to present the tragic and the comic scenes in as regular alternation as the layers of red and white in a side of streaky, well-cured bacon. The hero sinks upon his straw bed, weighed down by fetters and misfortunes; and, in the next scene, his faithful but unconscious squire regales the audience with a comic song. We behold with throbbing bosoms the heroine in the grasp of a proud and ruthless baron, her virtue and her life alike in danger, drawing forth her dagger to preserve the one at the cost of the other; and, just as our expectations are wrought up to the highest pitch, a whistle is heard, and we are straightway transported to the great hall of the castle, where a grey-headed seneschal sings a funny chorus with a funnier body of vassals, who are free of all sorts of places from church vaults to palaces, and roam about in company carolling perpetually.

Such changes appear absurd; but they are not so unnatural as they would seem at first sight. The transitions in real life from well-spread boards to death-beds, and from mourning weeds to holiday garments, are not a whit less startling, only there we are busy actors instead of passive lookers-on, which makes a vast difference. The actors in the mimic life of the theatre are blind to violent transitions and abrupt impulses of passion or feeling, which, presented before the eyes of mere spectators, are at once condemned as outrageous and preposterous.

As sudden shiftings of the scene, and rapid changes of time and place, are not only sanctioned in books by long usage, but are by many considered as the great art of authorship,—an author's skill in his craft being by such critics chiefly estimated with relation to the dilemmas in which he leaves his characters at the end of every chapter,—this brief introduction to the present one may perhaps be deemed unnecessary. If so, let it be considered a delicate intimation on the part of the historian that he is going back directly to the town in which Oliver Twist was born; the reader taking it for granted that there are good and substantial reasons for making the journey, or he would not be invited to proceed upon such an expedition on any account.

Mr. Bumble emerged at early morning from the workhouse gate, and walked, with portly carriage and commanding steps, up the High-street. He was in the full bloom and pride of beadleism; his cocked hat and coat were dazzling in the morning sun, and he clutched his cane with the vigorous tenacity of health and power. Mr. Bumble always carried his head high, but this morning it was higher than usual; there was an abstraction in his eye, and an elevation in his air, which might have warned an observant stranger that thoughts were passing in the beadle's mind, too great for utterance.

Mr. Bumble stopped not to converse with the small shop-keepers and others who spoke to him deferentially as he passed along. He merely returned their salutations with a wave of his hand, and relaxed not in his dignified pace until he reached the farm where Mrs. Mann tended the infant paupers with a parish care.

"Drat that beadle!" said Mrs. Mann, hearing the well-known impatient shaking at the garden gate. "If it isn't him at this time in the morning!—Lauk, Mr. Bumble, only think of its being you! Well, dear me, it *is* a pleasure this is! Come into the parlour, sir, please."

The first sentence was addressed to Susan, and the exclamations of delight were spoken to Mr. Bumble as the good lady unlocked the garden gate, and showed him with great attention and respect into the house.

"Mrs. Mann," said Mr. Bumble,—not sitting upon, or dropping himself into a seat, as any common jackanapes would, but letting himself

gradually and slowly down into a chair,—
" Mrs. Mann, ma'am, good morning!"

" Well, and good morning to you, sir," replied Mrs. Mann, with many smiles; " and hoping you find yourself well, sir?"

" So-so, Mrs. Mann," replied the beadle. " A porochial life is not a bed of roses, Mrs. Mann."

" Ah, that it isn't indeed, Mr. Bumble," rejoined the lady. And all the infant paupers might have chorused the rejoinder with great propriety if they had heard it.

" A porochial life, ma'am," continued Mr. Bumble, striking the table with his cane, " is a life of worry, and vexation, and hardihood; but all public characters, as I may say, must suffer prosecution."

Mrs. Mann, not very well knowing what the beadle meant, raised her hands with a look of sympathy, and sighed.

" Ah! You may well sigh, Mrs. Mann!" said the beadle.

Finding she had done right, Mrs. Mann sighed again, evidently to the satisfaction of the public character, who, repressing a complacent smile by looking sternly at his cocked hat, said,

"Mrs. Mann, I am a-going to London."

"Lauk, Mr. Bumble!" said Mrs. Mann, starting back.

"To London, ma'am," resumed the inflexible beadle, "by coach; I and two paupers, Mrs. Mann. A legal action is coming on about a settlement, and the board has appointed me—me, Mrs. Mann—to depose to the matter before the quarter-sessions at Clerkinwell; and I very much question," added Mr. Bumble, drawing himself up, "whether the Clerkinwell Sessions will not find themselves in the wrong box before they have done with me."

"Oh! you mustn't be too hard upon them, sir," said Mrs. Mann coaxingly.

"The Clerkinwell Sessions have brought it upon themselves, ma'am," replied Mr. Bumble; "and if the Clerkinwell Sessions find that they come off rather worse than they expected, the Clerkinwell Sessions have only themselves to thank."

There was so much determination and depth of purpose about the menacing manner in which Mr. Bumble delivered himself of these words, that Mrs. Mann appeared quite awed by them. At length she said,

"You're going by coach, sir? I thought it was always usual to send them paupers in carts."

"That's when they're ill, Mrs. Mann," said the beadle. "We put the sick paupers into open carts in the rainy weather, to prevent their taking cold."

"Oh!" said Mrs. Mann.

"The opposition coach contracts for these two, and takes them cheap," said Mr. Bumble. "They are both in a very low state, and we find it would come two pound cheaper to move 'em than to bury 'em,—that is, if we can throw 'em upon another parish, which I think we shall be able to do, if they don't die upon the road to spite us. Ha! ha! ha!"

When Mr. Bumble had laughed a little while, his eyes again encountered the cocked hat, and he became grave.

"We are forgetting business, ma'am," said the beadle;—" here is your porochial stipend for the month."

Wherewith Mr. Bumble produced some silver money, rolled up in paper, from his pocket-book, and requested a receipt, which Mrs. Mann wrote.

"It's very much blotted, sir," said the farmer of infants; "but it's formal enough, I dare say. Thank you, Mr. Bumble, sir; I am very much obliged to you, I'm sure."

Mr. Bumble nodded blandly in acknowledgment of Mrs. Mann's curtsey, and inquired how the children were.

"Bless their dear little hearts!" said Mrs. Mann with emotion, "they're as well as can be, the dears! Of course, except the two that died last week, and little Dick."

"Isn't that boy no better?" inquired Mr. Bumble. Mrs. Mann shook her head.

"He's a ill-conditioned, vicious, bad-disposed porochial child that," said Mr. Bumble angrily. "Where is he?"

"I'll bring him to you in one minute, sir," replied Mrs. Mann. "Here, you Dick!"

After some calling, Dick was discovered; and having had his face put under the pump, and dried upon Mrs. Mann's gown, he was led into the awful presence of Mr. Bumble, the beadle.

The child was pale and thin; his cheeks were sunken, and his eyes large and bright. The scanty parish dress, the livery of his misery, hung loosely upon his feeble body; and his young limbs had wasted away like those of an old man.

Such was the little being who stood trembling beneath Mr. Bumble's glance, not daring to lift his eyes from the floor, and dreading even to hear the beadle's voice.

"Can't you look at the gentleman, you obstinate boy?" said Mrs. Mann.

The child meekly raised his eyes, and encountered those of Mr. Bumble.

"What's the matter with you, porochial Dick?" inquired Mr. Bumble with well-timed jocularity.

"Nothing, sir," replied the child faintly.

"I should think not," said Mrs. Mann, who had of course laughed very much at Mr. Bumble's exquisite humour. "You want for nothing, I'm sure."

"I should like—" faltered the child.

"Hey-day!" interposed Mrs. Mann, "I suppose you're going to say that you *do* want for something, now? Why, you little wretch—"

"Stop, Mrs. Mann, stop!" said the beadle, raising his hand with a show of authority. "Like what, sir; eh?"

"I should like," faltered the child, "if somebody that can write, would put a few words down for me on a piece of paper, and fold it up, and seal it, and keep it for me after I am laid in the ground."

"Why, what does the boy mean?" exclaimed Mr. Bumble, on whom the earnest manner and wan aspect of the child had made some impression, accustomed as he was to such things. "What do you mean, sir?"

"I should like," said the child, "to leave my dear love to poor Oliver Twist, and to let him know how often I have sat by myself and cried to think of his wandering about in the dark nights with nobody to help him; and I should like to tell him," said the child, pressing his small hands together, and speaking with great fervour, "that I was glad to die when I was very young; for, perhaps, if I lived to be a man, and grew old, my little sister, who is in heaven, might forget me, or be unlike me; and it would be so much happier if we were both children there together."

Mr. Bumble surveyed the little speaker from head to foot with indescribable astonishment, and, turning to his companion, said, "They're all in one story, Mrs. Mann. That out-dacious Oliver has demoralized them all!"

"I couldn't have believed it, sir!" said Mrs. Mann, holding up her hands, and looking malignantly at Dick. "I never see such a hardened little wretch!"

"Take him away, ma'am!" said Mr. Bumble imperiously. "This must be stated to the board, Mrs. Mann."

"I hope the gentlemen will understand that it isn't my fault, sir?" said Mrs. Mann, whimpering pathetically.

"They shall understand that, ma'am; they shall be acquainted with the true state of the case," said Mr. Bumble pompously. "There; take him away. I can't bear the sight of him."

Dick was immediately taken away, and locked up in the coal-cellar; and Mr. Bumble shortly afterwards took himself off to prepare for his journey.

At six o'clock next morning, Mr. Bumble having exchanged his cocked hat for a round one, and encased his person in a blue great-coat with a cape to it, took his place on the outside of the coach, accompanied by the criminals whose settlement was disputed, with whom, in due course of time, he arrived in London, having experienced no other crosses by the way than those which originated in the perverse behaviour of the two paupers, who persisted in shivering, and complaining of the cold in a manner which, Mr. Bumble declared, caused his teeth to chatter in his head, and made him feel quite uncomfortable, although he had a great-coat on.

Having disposed of these evil-minded persons for the night, Mr. Bumble sat himself down in the house at which the coach stopped, and took a temperate dinner of steaks, oyster-sauce, and porter. Putting a glass of hot gin-and-water on the mantel-piece, he drew his chair to the fire, and, with sundry moral reflections on the too-prevalent sin of discontent and complaining, he then composed himself comfortably to read the paper.

The very first paragraph upon which Mr. Bumble's eyes rested, was the following advertisement.

"FIVE GUINEAS REWARD.

"Whereas a young boy, named Oliver Twist, absconded, or was enticed, on Thursday evening last, from his home at Pentonville, and has not since been heard of; the above reward will be paid to any person who will give such information as may lead to the discovery of the said Oliver Twist, or tend to throw any light upon his previous history, in which the advertiser is for many reasons warmly interested."

And then followed a full description of Oliver's dress, person, appearance, and disappearance, with the name and address of Mr. Brownlow at full length.

Mr. Bumble opened his eyes, read the advertisement slowly and carefully three several times, and in something more than five minutes was on his way to Pentonville, having actually in his excitement left the glass of hot gin-and-water untasted on the mantel-piece.

"Is Mr. Brownlow at home?" inquired Mr. Bumble of the girl who opened the door.

To this inquiry the girl returned the not uncommon, but rather evasive reply of, "I don't know—where do you come from?"

Mr. Bumble no sooner uttered Oliver's name in explanation of his errand, than Mrs. Bedwin, who had been listening at the parlour-door, hastened into the passage in a breathless state.

"Come in—come in," said the old lady: "I knew we should hear of him. Poor dear! I knew we should,—I was certain of it. Bless his heart! I said so all along."

Having said this, the worthy old lady hurried

back into the parlour again, and, seating herself on a sofa, burst into tears. The girl, who was not quite so susceptible, had run up-stairs meanwhile, and now returned with a request that Mr. Bumble would follow her immediately, which he did.

He was shown into the little back study, where sat Mr. Brownlow and his friend Mr. Grimwig, with decanters and glasses before them. The latter gentleman eyed him closely, and at once burst into the exclamation,

"A beadle—a parish beadle, or I'll eat my head!"

"Pray don't interrupt just now," said Mr. Brownlow. "Take a seat, will you?"

Mr. Bumble sat himself down, quite confounded by the oddity of Mr. Grimwig's manner. Mr. Brownlow moved the lamp so as to obtain an uninterrupted view of the beadle's countenance, and said with a little impatience,

"Now, sir, you come in consequence of having seen the advertisement?"

"Yes, sir," said Mr. Bumble.

"And you *are* a beadle, are you not?" inquired Mr. Grimwig.

"I am a porochial beadle, gentlemen," rejoined Mr. Bumble proudly.

"Of course," observed Mr. Grimwig aside to his friend. "I knew he was. His greatcoat is a parochial cut, and he looks a beadle all over."

Mr. Brownlow gently shook his head to impose silence on his friend, and resumed:

"Do you know where this poor boy is now?"

"No more than nobody," replied Mr. Bumble.

"Well, what *do* you know of him?" inquired the old gentleman. "Speak out, my friend, if you have anything to say. What do you know of him?"

"You don't happen to know any good of him, do you?" said Mr. Grimwig caustically, after an attentive perusal of Mr. Bumble's features.

Mr. Bumble caught at the inquiry very quickly, and shook his head with portentous solemnity.

"You see this?" said Mr. Grimwig, looking triumphantly at Mr. Brownlow.

Mr. Brownlow looked apprehensively at Bumble's pursed-up countenance, and requested him to communicate what he knew regarding Oliver, in as few words as possible.

Mr. Bumble put down his hat, unbuttoned his coat, folded his arms, inclined his head in a retrospective manner, and, after a few moments' reflection, commenced his story.

It would be tedious if given in the beadle's words, occupying as it did some twenty minutes in the telling; but the sum and substance of it was, that Oliver was a foundling, born of low and vicious parents, who had from his birth displayed no better qualities than treachery, ingratitude, and malice, and who had terminated his brief career in the place of his birth, by making a sanguinary and cowardly attack on an unoffending lad, and running away in the night-time from his master's house. In proof of his really being the person he represented himself, Mr. Bumble laid upon the table the papers he had brought to town, and, folding his arms again, awaited Mr. Brownlow's observations.

"I fear it is all too true," said the old gentleman sorrowfully, after looking over the papers. "This is not much for your intelligence; but I would gladly have given you treble the money, if it had been favourable to the boy."

It is not at all improbable that if Mr. Bumble had been possessed with this information at an earlier period of the interview, he might have imparted a very different colouring to his little history. It was too late to do it now, however; so he shook his head gravely, and, pocketing the five guineas, withdrew.

Mr. Brownlow paced the room to and fro for some minutes, evidently so much disturbed by the beadle's tale, that even Mr. Grimwig forbore to vex him further. At length he stopped, and rang the bell violently.

"Mrs. Bedwin," said Mr. Brownlow when the housekeeper appeared, "that boy, Oliver, is an impostor."

"It can't be, sir; it cannot be," said the old lady energetically.

"I tell you he is," retorted the old gentleman sharply. "What do you mean by 'can't be'? We have just heard a full account of him from his birth, and he has been a thorough-paced little villain all his life."

"I never will believe it, sir," replied the old lady, firmly.

"You old women never believe anything but quack-doctors and lying story-books," growled Mr. Grimwig. "I knew it all along. Why didn't you take my advice in the beginning; you would if he hadn't had a fever, I suppose,—eh? He was interesting, wasn't he? Interesting! Bah!" and Mr. Grimwig poked the fire with a flourish.

"He was a dear, grateful, gentle child, sir," retorted Mrs. Bedwin indignantly. "I know what children are, sir, and have done these forty years; and people who can't say the same shouldn't say anything about them—that's my opinion."

This was a hard hit at Mr. Grimwig, who was a bachelor; but as it extorted nothing from that gentleman but a smile, the old lady tossed her head and smoothed down her apron preparatory to another speech, when she was stopped by Mr. Brownlow.

" Silence !" said the old gentleman, feigning an anger he was far from feeling. " Never let me hear the boy's name again : I rang to tell you that. Never — never, on any pretence, mind. You may leave the room, Mrs. Bedwin. Remember; I am in earnest."

There were sad hearts at Mr. Brownlow's that night. Oliver's sunk within him when he thought of his good kind friends; but it was well for him that he could not know what they had heard, or it would have broken outright.

CHAPTER XVIII.

HOW OLIVER PASSED HIS TIME IN THE IMPROVING SOCIETY OF HIS REPUTABLE FRIENDS.

About noon next day, when the Dodger and Master Bates had gone out to pursue their customary avocations, Mr. Fagin took the opportunity of reading Oliver a long lecture on the crying sin of ingratitude, of which he clearly demonstrated he had been guilty to no ordinary extent in wilfully absenting himself from the society of his anxious friends, and still more in endeavouring to escape from them after so much trouble and expense had been incurred in his recovery. Mr. Fagin laid great stress on the fact of his having taken Oliver in and cherished him, when without his timely aid he might have perished with hunger; and related the dismal and affecting history of a young lad whom in his philanthropy he had succoured under parallel circumstances, but who, proving unworthy of his confidence, and evincing a desire to communicate with the police, had unfortunately come to be hung at the Old Bailey one morning. Mr. Fagin did not seek to conceal his share in the catastrophe, but lamented with tears in his eyes that the wrong-headed and treacherous behaviour of the young person in question had rendered it necessary that he should become the victim of certain evidence for the crown, which, if it were not precisely true, was indispensably necessary for the safety of him (Mr. Fagin) and a few select friends. Mr. Fagin concluded by drawing a rather disagreeable picture of the discomforts of hanging, and, with great friendliness and politeness of manner, expressed his anxious hope that he might never be obliged to submit Oliver Twist to that unpleasant operation.

Little Oliver's blood ran cold as he listened to the Jew's words, and imperfectly comprehended the dark threats conveyed in them. That it was possible even for justice itself to confound the innocent with the guilty when they were in accidental companionship, he knew already; and that deeply-laid plans for the destruction of inconveniently-knowing, or over-communicative persons, had been really devised and carried out by the old Jew on more occasions than one, he thought by no means unlikely when he recollected the general nature of the altercations between that gentleman and Mr. Sikes, which seemed to bear reference to some foregone conspiracy of the kind. As he glanced timidly up, and met the Jew's searching look, he felt that his pale face and trembling limbs were neither unnoticed, nor unrelished, by the wary villain.

The Jew smiled hideously, and, patting Oliver on the head, said that if he kept himself quiet, and applied himself to business, he saw they would be very good friends yet. Then taking his hat, and covering himself up in an old patched great-coat, he went out and locked the room-door behind him.

And so Oliver remained all that day, and for the greater part of many subsequent days, seeing nobody between early morning and midnight, and left during the long hours to commune with his own thoughts; which never failing to revert to his kind friends, and the opinion they must long ago have formed of him, were sad indeed. After the lapse of a week or so, the Jew left the room-door unlocked, and he was at liberty to wander about the house.

It was a very dirty place; but the rooms up stairs had great high wooden mantel-pieces and large doors, with paneled walls and cornices to the ceilings, which, although they were black with neglect and dust, were ornamented in various ways; from all of which tokens Oliver concluded that a long time ago, before the old Jew was born, it had belonged to better people, and had perhaps been quite gay and handsome, dismal and dreary as it looked now.

Spiders had built their webs in the angles of the walls and ceilings; and sometimes, when

Oliver walked softly into a room, the mice would scamper across the floor, and run back terrified to their holes. With these exceptions, there was neither sight nor sound of any living thing; and often, when it grew dark, and he was tired of wandering from room to room, he would crouch in the corner of the passage by the street-door, to be as near living people as he could, and remain there listening and counting the hours until the Jew or the boys returned.

In all the rooms the mouldering shutters were fast closed, and the bars which held them were screwed tight into the wood; the only light which was admitted making its way through round holes at the top, which made the rooms more gloomy, and filled them with strange shadows. There was a back-garret window, with rusty bars outside, which had no shutter, and out of which Oliver often gazed with a melancholy face for hours together; but nothing was to be descried from it but a confused and crowded mass of house-tops, blacken-ed chimneys, and gable-ends. Sometimes, indeed, a ragged grizzly head might be seen peering over the parapet-wall of a distant house, but it was quickly withdrawn again; and as the window of Oliver's observatory was nailed down, and dimmed with the rain and smoke of years, it was as much as he could do to make out the forms of the different objects beyond, without making any attempt to be seen or heard,— which he had as much chance of being as if he had been inside the ball of St. Paul's Cathedral.

One afternoon, the Dodger and Master Bates being engaged out that evening, the first-named young gentleman took it into his head to evince some anxiety regarding the decoration of his person (which, to do him justice, was by no means an habitual weakness with him;) and, with this end and aim, he condescendingly commanded Oliver to assist him in his toilet straightway.

Oliver was but too glad to make himself useful; too happy to have some faces, however bad, to look upon, and too desirous to conciliate those about him when he could honestly do so, to throw any objection in the way of this proposal; so he at once expressed his readiness, and, kneeling on the floor, while the Dodger sat upon the table so that he could take his foot in his lap, he applied himself to a process which Mr. Dawkins designated as "japanning his trotter-cases," and which phrase, rendered into plain English, signifieth cleaning his boots.

Whether it was the sense of freedom and independence which a rational animal may be supposed to feel when he sits on a table in an easy attitude, smoking a pipe, swinging one leg carelessly to and fro, and having his boots cleaned all the time, without even the past trouble of having taken them off, or the prospective misery of putting them on, to disturb his reflections; or whether it was the goodness of the tobacco that soothed the feelings of the Dodger, or the mildness of the beer that mollified his thoughts, he was evidently tinctured for the nonce with a spice of romance and enthusiasm foreign to his general nature. He looked down on Oliver with a thoughtful countenance for a brief space, and then, raising his head, and heaving a gentle sigh, said, half in abstraction, and half to Master Bates,

" What a pity it is he isn't a prig!"

" Ah!" said Master Charles Bates; " he don't know what 's good for him."

The Dodger sighed again, and resumed his pipe, as did Charley Bates. They both smoked for some seconds in silence.

" I suppose you don't even know what a prig is?" said the Dodger mournfully.

" I think I know that," replied Oliver, hastily looking up. " It 's a th—; you 're one, are you not?" inquired Oliver, checking himself.

" I am," replied the Dodger. " I 'd scorn to be anythink else." Mr. Dawkins gave his hat a ferocious cock after delivering this sentiment, and looked at Master Bates as if to denote that he would feel obliged by his saying anything to the contrary. " I am," repeated the Dodger; " so 's Charley, so 's Fagin, so 's Sikes, so 's Nancy, so 's Bet, so we all are, down to the dog, and he's the downiest one of the lot."

"And the least given to peaching," added Charley Bates.

"He wouldn't so much as bark in a witness-box for fear of committing himself; no, not if you tied him up in one, and left him there without wittles for a fortnight," said the Dodger.

"That he wouldn't; not a bit of it," observed Charley.

"He's a rum dog. Don't he look fierce at any strange cove that laughs or sings when he's in company!" pursued the Dodger. "Won't he growl at all when he hears a fiddle playing, and don't he hate other dogs as ain't of his breed!—Oh, no!"

"He's an out-and-out Christian," said Charley.

This was merely intended as a tribute to the animal's abilities, but it was an appropriate remark in another sense, if Master Bates had only known it; for there are a great many ladies and gentlemen claiming to be out-and-out Christians, between whom and Mr. Sikes's dog there exist very strong and singular points of resemblance.

"Well, well," said the Dodger, recurring to the point from which they had strayed, with that mindfulness of his profession which influenced all his proceedings. "This hasn't got anything to do with young Green here."

"No more it has," said Charley. "Why don't you put yourself under Fagin, Oliver?"

"And make your fortun' out of hand?" added the Dodger, with a grin.

"And so be able to retire on your property, and do the gen-teel, as I mean to in the very next leap-year but four that ever comes, and the forty-second Tuesday in Trinity-week," said Charley Bates.

"I don't like it," rejoined Oliver timidly; "I wish they would let me go. I—I—would rather go."

"And Fagin would *rather* not!" rejoined Charley.

Oliver knew this too well; but, thinking it

might be dangerous to express his feelings more openly, he only sighed, and went on with his boot-cleaning.

"Go!" exclaimed the Dodger. "Why, where's your spirit? Don't you take any pride out of yourself? Would you go and be dependent on your friends, eh?"

"Oh, blow that!" said Master Bates, drawing two or three silk handkerchiefs from his pocket, and tossing them into a cupboard, "that's too mean, that is."

"*I* couldn't do it," said the Dodger, with an air of haughty disgust.

"You can leave your friends, though," said Oliver with a half-smile, "and let them be punished for what you did."

"That," rejoined the Dodger, with a wave of his pipe,—"that was all out of consideration for Fagin, 'cause the traps know that we work together, and he might have got into trouble if we hadn't made our lucky; that was the move, wasn't it, Charley?"

Master Bates nodded assent, and would have

spoken, but that the recollection of Oliver's flight came so suddenly upon him, that the smoke he was inhaling got entangled with a laugh, and went up into his head, and down into his throat, and brought on a fit of coughing and stamping about five minutes long.

"Look here," said the Dodger, drawing forth a handful of shillings and halfpence. "Here's a jolly life!—what's the odds where it comes from? Here, catch hold; there's plenty more where they were took from. You won't, won't you?—Oh, you precious flat!"

"It's naughty, ain't it, Oliver?" inquired Charley Bates. "He'll come to be scragged, won't he?"

"I don't know what that means," replied Oliver, looking round.

"Something in this way, old feller," said Charley. As he said it, Master Bates caught up an end of his neckerchief, and, holding it erect in the air, dropped his head on his shoulder, and jerked a curious sound through his teeth, thereby indicating, by a lively pantomi-

mic representation, that scragging and hanging were one and the same thing.

"That's what it means," said Charley. "Look how he stares, Jack. I never did see such prime company as that 'ere boy; he'll be the death of me, I know he will." And Master Charles Bates, having laughed heartily again, resumed his pipe with tears in his eyes.

"You've been brought up bad," said the Dodger, surveying his boots with much satisfaction when Oliver had polished them. "Fagin will make something of you, though, or you'll be the first he ever had that turned out unprofitable. You'd better begin at once, for you'll come to the trade long before you think of it, and you're only losing time, Oliver."

Master Bates backed this advice with sundry moral admonitions of his own, which being exhausted, he and his friend Mr. Dawkins launched into a glowing description of the numerous pleasures incidental to the life they led, interspersed with a variety of hints to Oliver that the best thing he could do, would be to secure Fagin's favour without more delay by the same means which they had employed to gain it.

"And always put this in your pipe, Nolly," said the Dodger, as the Jew was heard unlocking the door above, "if you don't take fogles and tickers——"

"What's the good of talking in that way?" interposed Master Bates: "he don't know what you mean."

"If you don't take pocket-hankechers and watches," said the Dodger, reducing his conversation to the level of Oliver's capacity, "some other cove will; so that the coves that lose 'em will be all the worse, and you'll be all the worse too, and nobody half a ha'p'orth the better, except the chaps wot gets them — and you've just as good a right to them as they have."

"To be sure,—to be sure!" said the Jew, who had entered unseen by Oliver. "It all lies in a nutshell, my dear—in a nutshell, take the Dodger's word for it. Ha! ha!—he understands the catechism of his trade."

The old man rubbed his hands gleefully together as he corroborated the Dodger's reasoning in these terms, and chuckled with delight at his pupil's proficiency.

The conversation proceeded no farther at this time, for the Jew had returned home accompanied by Miss Betsy, and a gentleman whom Oliver had never seen before, but who was accosted by the Dodger as Tom Chitling, and who, having lingered on the stairs to exchange a few gallantries with the lady, now made his appearance.

Mr. Chitling was older in years than the Dodger, having perhaps numbered eighteen winters; but there was a degree of deference in his deportment towards that young gentleman which seemed to indicate that he felt himself conscious of a slight inferiority in point of genius and professional acquirements. He had small twinkling eyes, and a pock-marked face;

wore a fur cap, a dark corduroy jacket, greasy fustian trousers, and an apron. His wardrobe was, in truth, rather out of repair; but he excused himself to the company by stating that his "time" was only out an hour before, and that, in consequence of having worn the regimentals for six weeks past, he had not been able to bestow any attention on his private clothes. Mr. Chitling added, with strong marks of irritation, that the new way of fumigating clothes up yonder was infernal unconstitutional, for it burnt holes in them, and there was no remedy against the county; the same remark he considered to apply to the regulation mode of cutting the hair, which he held to be decidedly unlawful. Mr. Chitling wound up his observations by stating that he had not touched a drop of anything for forty-two mortal long hard-working days, and that he "wished he might be busted if he wasn't as dry as a lime-basket."

"Where do you think the gentleman has come from, Oliver?" inquired the Jew with a grin, as the other boys put a bottle of spirits on the table.

"I—I—don't know, sir," replied Oliver.

"Who's that?" inquired Tom Chitling, casting a contemptuous look at Oliver.

"A young friend of mine, my dear," replied the Jew.

"He's in luck then," said the young man, with a meaning look at Fagin. "Never mind where I came from, young 'un; you'll find your way there soon enough, I'll bet a crown!"

At this sally the boys laughed, and, after some more jokes on the same subject, exchanged a few short whispers with Fagin, and withdrew.

After some words apart between the last comer and Fagin, they drew their chairs towards the fire; and the Jew, telling Oliver to come and sit by him, led the conversation to the topics most calculated to interest his hearers. These were, the great advantages of the trade, the proficiency of the Dodger, the amiability of

Charley Bates, and the liberality of the Jew himself. At length these subjects displayed signs of being thoroughly exhausted, and Mr. Chitling did the same (for the house of correction becomes fatiguing after a week or two); Miss Betsy accordingly withdrew, and left the party to their repose.

From this day Oliver was seldom left alone, but was placed in almost constant communication with the two boys, who played the old game with the Jew every day,—whether for their own improvement or Oliver's, Mr. Fagin best knew. At other times the old man would tell them stories of robberies he had committed in his younger days, mixed up with so much that was droll and curious, that Oliver could not help laughing heartily, and showing that he was amused in spite of all his better feelings.

In short, the wily old Jew had the boy in his toils; and, having prepared his mind, by solitude and gloom, to prefer any society to the companionship of his own sad thoughts in such a dreary place, was now slowly instilling into his soul the poison which he hoped would blacken it and change its hue for ever.

CHAPTER XIX.

IN WHICH A NOTABLE PLAN IS DISCUSSED AND DETERMINED ON.

It was a chill, damp, windy night, when the Jew, buttoning his great-coat tight round his shrivelled body, and pulling the collar up over his ears so as completely to obscure the lower part of his face, emerged from his den. He paused on the step as the door was locked and chained behind him; and having listened while the boys made all secure, and until their retreating footsteps were no longer audible, slunk down the street as quickly as he could.

The house to which Oliver had been conveyed was in the neighbourhood of Whitechapel; the Jew stopped for an instant at the corner of the street, and, glancing suspiciously round, crossed the road, and struck off in the direction of Spitalfields.

The mud lay thick upon the stones, and a black mist hung over the streets; the rain fell sluggishly down, and everything felt cold and clammy to the touch. It seemed just the night when it befitted such a being as the Jew to be abroad. As he glided stealthily along, creeping beneath the shelter of the walls and doorways, the hideous old man seemed like some loathsome reptile, engendered in the slime and darkness through which he moved, crawling forth by night in search of some rich offal for a meal.

He kept on his course through many winding and narrow ways until he reached Bethnal Green; then, turning suddenly off to the left, he soon became involved in a maze of the mean and dirty streets which abound in that close and densely-populated quarter.

The Jew was evidently too familiar with the ground he traversed, however, to be at all bewildered either by the darkness of the night or the intricacies of the way. He hurried through several alleys and streets, and at length turned into one lighted only by a single lamp at the farther end. At the door of a house in this street he knocked, and having exchanged a few muttered words with the person who opened the door, walked up stairs.

A dog growled as he touched the handle of a door, and a man's voice demanded who was there.

"Only me, Bill; only me, my dear," said the Jew, looking in.

"Bring in your body," said Sikes. "Lie down, you stupid brute. Don't you know the devil when he's got a great-coat on?"

Apparently the dog had been somewhat deceived by Mr. Fagin's outer garment; for as the Jew unbuttoned it, and threw it over the back of a chair, he retired to the corner from which he had risen, wagging his tail as he went, to show that he was as well satisfied as it was in his nature to be.

" Well !" said Sikes.

" Well, my dear," replied the Jew. " Ah! Nancy."

The latter recognition was uttered with just enough of embarrassment to imply a doubt of its reception; for Mr. Fagin and his young friend had not met since she had interfered in behalf of Oliver. All doubts upon the subject, if he had any, were speedily removed by the young lady's behaviour. She took her feet off the fender, pushed back her chair, and bade Fagin draw up his, without saying any more about it, for it was a cold night, and no mistake.

" It *is* cold, Nancy dear," said the Jew, as he warmed his skinny hands over the fire. " It seems to go right through one," added the old man, touching his left side.

" It must be a piercer if it finds its way through your heart," said Mr. Sikes. " Give him something to drink, Nancy. Burn my body, make haste. It's enough to turn a man ill to see his lean old carcase shivering in that way, like a ugly ghost just rose from the grave."

Nancy quickly brought a bottle from a cupboard in which there were many, which, to judge from the diversity of their appearance, were filled with several kinds of liquids; and Sikes, pouring out a glass of brandy, bade the Jew drink it off.

"Quite enough, quite, thankye, Bill," replied the Jew, putting down the glass after just setting his lips to it.

"What! you're afraid of our getting the better of you, are you?" inquired Sikes, fixing his eyes on the Jew: "ugh!"

With a hoarse grunt of contempt Mr. Sikes seized the glass and threw the remainder of its contents into the ashes, as a preparatory ceremony to filling it again for himself, which he did at once.

The Jew glanced round the room as his companion tossed down the second glassful; not in curiosity, for he had seen it often before, but in a restless and suspicious manner which was habitual to him. It was a meanly furnished apartment, with nothing but the contents of the closet to induce the belief that its occupier was anything but a working man; and with no more suspicious articles displayed to view than two or three heavy bludgeons which stood in a corner, and a " life-preserver" that hung over the mantelpiece.

"There," said Sikes, smacking his lips. "Now I'm ready."

"For business—eh?" inquired the Jew.

"For business," replied Sikes; "so say what you've got to say."

"About the crib at Chertsey, Bill?" said the Jew, drawing his chair forward, and speaking in a very low voice.

"Yes. Wot about it?" inquired Sikes.

"Ah! you know what I mean, my dear," said the Jew. "He knows what I mean, Nancy; don't he?"

"No, he don't," sneered Mr. Sikes, " or he won't, and that's the same thing. Speak out, and call things by their right names; don't sit there winking and blinking, and talking to me in hints, as if you warn't the very first that thought about the robbery. D— your eyes! wot d'ye mean?"

"Hush, Bill, hush!" said the Jew, who had in vain attempted to stop this burst of indignation; " somebody will hear us, my dear; somebody will hear us."

"Let 'em hear!" said Sikes; " I don't care." But as Mr. Sikes *did* care, upon reflection he dropped his voice as he said the words, and grew calmer.

"There, there," said the Jew coaxingly. "It was only my caution — nothing more. Now, my dear, about that crib at Chertsey, when is it to be done, Bill, eh?—when is it to be done? Such plate, my dears, such plate!" said the Jew, rubbing his hands, and elevating his eyebrows in a rapture of anticipation.

"Not at all," replied Sikes coldly.

"Not to be done at all!" echoed the Jew, leaning back in his chair.

"No, not at all," rejoined Sikes; "at least it can't be a put-up job, as we expected."

"Then it hasn't been properly gone about," said the Jew, turning pale with anger. "Don't tell me."

"But I will tell you," retorted Sikes. "Who are you that's not to be told? I tell you that Toby Crackit has been hanging about the place for a fortnight, and he can't get one of the servants into a line."

"Do you mean to tell me, Bill," said the Jew, softening as the other grew heated, "that neither of the two men in the house can be got over?"

"Yes, I do mean to tell you so," replied Sikes. "The old lady has had 'em these twenty year; and, if you were to give 'em five hundred pound, they wouldn't be in it."

"But do you mean to say, my dear," remonstrated the Jew, " that the women can't be got over?"

" Not a bit of it," replied Sikes.

" Not by flash Toby Crackit?" said the Jew incredulously. " Think what women are, Bill."

" No; not even by flash Toby Crackit," replied Sikes. " He says he's worn sham whiskers and a canary waistcoat the whole blessed time he's been loitering down there, and it's all of no use."

" He should have tried mustachios and a pair of military trousers, my dear," said the Jew, after a few moments' reflection.

" So he did," rejoined Sikes, " and they warn't of no more use than the other plant."

The Jew looked very blank at this information, and, arter ruminating for some minutes with his chin sunk on his breast, raised his head, and said with a deep sigh that, if flash Toby Crackit reported aright, he feared the game was up.

" And yet," said the old man, dropping his

hands on his knees, " it's a sad thing, my dear, to lose so much when we had set our hearts upon it."

" So it is," said Mr. Sikes; " worse luck!"

A long silence ensued, during which the Jew was plunged in deep thought, with his face wrinkled into an expression of villany perfectly demoniacal. Sikes eyed him furtively from time to time; and Nancy, apparently fearful of irritating the housebreaker, sat with her eyes fixed upon the fire, as if she had been deaf to all that passed.

" Fagin," said Sikes, abruptly breaking the stillness that prevailed, " is it worth fifty shiners extra, if it's safely done from the outside?"

" Yes," said the Jew, suddenly rousing himself, as if from a trance.

" Is it a bargain?" inquired Sikes.

" Yes, my dear, yes," rejoined the Jew, grasping the other's hand, his eyes glistening, and every muscle in his face working with the excitement that the inquiry had awakened.

"Then," said Sikes, thrusting aside the Jew's hand with some disdain, " let it come off as soon as you like. Toby and I were over the garden-wall the night afore last, sounding the panels of the door and shutters: the crib's barred up at night like a jail, but there's one part we can crack, safe and softly."

" Which is that, Bill?" asked the Jew eagerly.

" Why," whispered Sikes, " as you cross the lawn——"

" Yes, yes," said the Jew, bending his head forward, with his eyes almost starting out of it.

" Umph!" cried Sikes, stopping short as the girl, scarcely moving her head, looked suddenly round and pointed for an instant to the Jew's face. " Never mind which part it is. You can't do it without me, I know; but it's best to be on the safe side when one deals with you."

" As you like, my dear, as you like," replied the Jew, biting his lip. " Is there no help wanted but yours and Toby's?"

"None," said Sikes, "'cept a centre-bit and a boy. The first we've both got; the second you must find us."

"A boy!" exclaimed the Jew. "Oh! then it is a panel, eh?"

"Never mind wot it is!" replied Sikes; "I want a boy, and he mustn't be a big un. Lord!" said Mr. Sikes reflectively, "if I'd only got that young boy of Ned, the chimbley-sweeper's — he kept him small on purpose, and let him out by the job. But the father gets lagged, and then the Juvenile Delinquent Society comes, and takes the boy away from a trade where he was arning money, teaches him to read and write, and in time makes a 'prentice of him. And so they go on," said Mr. Sikes, his wrath rising with the recollection of his wrongs,—"so they go on; and, if they'd got money enough, (which it's a Providence they have not,) we shouldn't have half-a-dozen boys left in the whole trade in a year or two."

"No more we should," acquiesced the Jew,

who had been considering during this speech, and had only caught the last sentence. "Bill!"

"What now?" inquired Sikes.

The Jew nodded his head towards Nancy, who was still gazing at the fire, and intimated by a sign that he would have her told to leave the room. Sikes shrugged his shoulders impatiently, as if he thought the precaution unnecessary, but complied, nevertheless, by requesting Miss Nancy to fetch him a jug of beer.

"You don't want any beer," said Nancy, folding her arms, and retaining her seat very composedly.

"I tell you I do!" replied Sikes.

"Nonsense," rejoined the girl, coolly. "Go on, Fagin. I know what he's going to say, Bill; he needn't mind me."

The Jew still hesitated, and Sikes looked from one to the other in some surprise.

"Why, you don't mind the old girl, do you, Fagin?" he asked at length. "You've known her long enough to trust her, or the devil's in it. She ain't one to blab, are you, Nancy?"

"*I* should think not!" replied the young lady, drawing her chair up to the table, and putting her elbows upon it.

"No, no, my dear,—I know you're not," said the Jew; "but——" and again the old man paused.

"But wot?" inquired Sikes.

"I didn't know whether she mightn't p'r'aps be out of sorts, you know, my dear, as she was the other night," replied the Jew.

At this confession Miss Nancy burst into a loud laugh, and, swallowing a glass of brandy, shook her head with an air of defiance, and burst into sundry exclamations of "Keep the game a-going!" "Never say die!" and the like, which seemed at once to have the effect of re-assuring both gentlemen, for the Jew nodded his head with a satisfied air, and resumed his seat, as did Mr. Sikes likewise.

"Now, Fagin," said Nancy with a laugh, "tell Bill at once about Oliver!"

"Ah! you're a clever one, my dear; the

sharpest girl I ever saw!" said the Jew, patting her on the neck. " It *was* about Oliver I was going to speak, sure enough. Ha! ha! ha!"

" What about him?" demanded Sikes.

" He's the boy for you, my dear," replied the Jew in a hoarse whisper, laying his finger on the side of his nose, and grinning frightfully.

" He!" exclaimed Sikes.

" Have him, Bill!" said Nancy. " I would if I was in your place. He mayn't be so much up as any of the others; but that's not what you want if he's only to open a door for you. Depend upon it he's a safe one, Bill."

" I know he is," rejoined Fagin; " he's been in good training these last few weeks, and it's time he began to work for his bread. Besides, the others are all too big."

" Well, he is just the size I want," said Mr. Sikes, ruminating.

" And will do everything you want, Bill, my dear," interposed the Jew; "he can't help himself,—that is if you only frighten him enough."

"Frighten him!" echoed Sikes. "It'll be no sham frightening, mind you. If there's anything queer about him when we once get into the work,—in for a penny, in for a pound,—you won't see him alive again, Fagin. Think of that before you send him. Mark my words," said the robber, poising a heavy crowbar which he had drawn from under the bedstead.

"I've thought of it all," said the Jew with energy. "I've—I've had my eye upon him, my dears, close—close. Once let him feel that he is one of us; once fill his mind with the idea that he has been a thief, and he's ours,—ours for his life! Oho! It couldn't have come about better!" The old man crossed his arms upon his breast, and, drawing his head and shoulders into a heap, literally hugged himself for joy.

"Ours!" said Sikes. "Yours, you mean."

"Perhaps I do, my dear," said the Jew with a shrill chuckle. "Mine, if you like, Bill."

"And wot," said Sikes, scowling fiercely on

his agreeable friend,—" wot makes you take so much pains about one chalk-faced kid, when you know there are fifty boys snoozing about Common Garden every night, as you might pick and choose from?"

"Because they're of no use to me, my dear," replied the Jew with some confusion, "not worth the taking; for their looks convict 'em when they get into trouble, and I lose 'em all. With this boy properly managed, my dears, I could do what I couldn't with twenty of them. Besides," said the Jew, recovering his self-possession, "he has us now if he could only give us leg-bail again; and he *must* be in the same boat with us. Never mind how he came there, it's quite enough for my power over him that he was in a robbery, that's all I want. Now how much better this is than being obliged to put the poor leetle boy out of the way, which would be dangerous, and we should lose by it besides."

"When is it to be done?" asked Nancy,

stopping some turbulent exclamation on the part of Mr. Sikes, expressive of the disgust with which he received Fagin's affectation of humanity.

" Ah, to be sure," said the Jew, " when is it to be done, Bill ?"

" I planned with Toby, the night arter to-morrow," rejoined Sikes in a surly voice, " if he heard nothing from me to the contrairy."

" Good," said the Jew; " there's no moon."

" No," rejoined Sikes.

" It's all arranged about bringing off the swag,* is it ?" asked the Jew.

Sikes nodded.

" And about——"

" Oh, ah, it's all planned," rejoined Sikes, interrupting him; " never mind particulars. You'd better bring the boy here to-morrow night; I shall get off the stones an hour arter day-break. Then you hold your tongue, and keep the melting-pot ready, and that's all you'll have to do."

* Booty.

After some discussion, in which all three took an active part, it was decided that Nancy should repair to the Jew's next evening when the night had set in, and bring Oliver away with her: Fagin craftily observing, that, if he evinced any disinclination to the task, he would be more willing to accompany the girl who had so recently interfered in his behalf, than anybody else. It was also solemnly arranged that poor Oliver should, for the purposes of the contemplated expedition, be unreservedly consigned to the care and custody of Mr. William Sikes; and further, that the said Sikes should deal with him as he thought fit, and should not be held responsible by the Jew for any mischance or evil that might befall the boy, or any punishment with which it might be necessary to visit him, it being understood that, to render the compact in this respect binding, any representations made by Mr. Sikes on his return should be required to be confirmed and corroborated, in all important particulars, by the testimony of flash Toby Crackit.

These preliminaries adjusted, Mr. Sikes proceeded to drink brandy at a furious rate, and to flourish the crowbar in an alarming manner, yelling forth at the same time most unmusical snatches of song, mingled with wild execrations. At length, in a fit of professional enthusiasm, he insisted upon producing his box of housebreaking tools, which he had no sooner stumbled in with, and opened for the purpose of explaining the nature and properties of the various implements it contained, and the peculiar beauties of their construction, than he fell over it upon the floor, and went to sleep where he fell.

" Good night, Nancy," said the Jew, muffling himself up as before.

" Good night."

Their eyes met, and the Jew scrutinised her narrowly. There was no flinching about the girl. She was as true and earnest in the matter as Toby Crackit himself could be.

The Jew again bade her good night, and, bestowing a sly kick upon the prostrate form of

Mr. Sikes while her back was turned, groped down stairs.

"Always the way," muttered the Jew to himself as he turned homewards. "The worst of these women is, that a very little thing serves to call up some long-forgotten feeling; and the best of them is, that it never lasts. Ha! ha! The man against the child, for a bag of gold!"

Beguiling the time with these pleasant reflections, Mr. Fagin wended his way through mud and mire to his gloomy abode, where the Dodger was sitting up, impatiently awaiting his return.

"Is Oliver a-bed? I want to speak to him," was his first remark as they descended the stairs.

"Hours ago," replied the Dodger, throwing open a door. "Here he is!"

The boy was lying fast asleep on a rude bed upon the floor: so pale with anxiety and sadness, and the closeness of his prison, that he looked like death; not death as it shows in shroud and coffin, but in the guise it wears when life has just departed; when a young and gentle spirit has but an instant fled to heaven, and the gross air of the world has not had time to breathe upon the changing dust it hallowed.

"Not now," said the Jew, turning softly, away. "To-morrow. To-morrow."

END OF THE FIRST VOLUME.

LONDON:
PRINTED BY SAMUEL BENTLEY,
Dorset Street, Fleet Street.

NEW WORKS OF ENTERTAINMENT

EDITED BY

CHARLES DICKENS, ESQ. (BOZ.)

Author of "Oliver Twist," "The Pickwick Papers," &c.

I.

LIFE OF GRIMALDI THE CLOWN.

WITH TWELVE COMIC ILLUSTRATIONS BY GEORGE CRUIKSHANK.

Two Volumes, with Portrait, price 21s.

II.

BENTLEY'S MISCELLANY.

PUBLISHING IN MONTHLY NUMBERS.

PRICE HALF-A-CROWN.

ILLUSTRATED BY GEORGE CRUIKSHANK,

Volumes I. II. and III. of this work are now completed, and may be had, together or separately, price 16s. each. The volumes, which are handsomely bound, respectively contain upwards of Six Hundred pages of letter-press, embellished with numerous ILLUSTRATIONS by GEORGE CRUIKSHANK, Portraits, &c. and

COMPRISE ORIGINAL CONTRIBUTIONS BY THE FOLLOWING DISTINGUISHED WRITERS:—

CHARLES DICKENS, ESQ. "BOZ" (THE EDITOR).

Thomas Ingoldsby, Esq.
Dr. Maginn.
Theodore Hook, Esq.
T. Haynes Bayly, Esq.
Author of "Rattlin the Reefer."
W. H. Maxwell, Esq. Author of "Stories of Waterloo."
William Jerdan, Esq.
Samuel Lover, Esq.
Miss Louisa Sheridan.
Author of "Headlong Hall."
'Joyce Jocund.'
George Hogarth, Esq.
J. Fenimore Cooper, Esq. Author of "The Pilot."
Captain Medwin.
Author of "Confessions of an Elderly Gentleman."
Charles Whitehead, Esq.
Dr. Millingen.

Colonel Napier.
J. Sheridan Knowles, Esq.
Mrs. C. Gore.
James Morier, Esq.
W. B. Le Gros, Esq.
'Father Prout.'
Mark Lemon.
'Dalton.'
J. A. Wade, Esq.
'The Old Sailor.'
Author of "The Bashful Irishman."
C. Dance.
Paul de Kock.
Author of "Tales of an Antiquary."
J. Hamilton Reynolds.
Thomas Raikes, Esq. (Author of "The City of the Czar.")
Richard Johns, Esq.

RICHARD BENTLEY, NEW BURLINGTON STREET.

TO BE HAD AT ALL THE LIBRARIES

THE NEW NOVELS JUST PUBLISHED.

I.

MELTON DE MOWBRAY; OR, THE BANKER'S SON.

Three Volumes.

"There is considerable power and a close observation of life manifested in this work. The description of London life in the brilliant age of Fox, Pitt, and Sheridan, (whose portraits are incidentally sketched by the author with a vigorous hand,) is remarkable for its fidelity and liveliness. It is an amusing and clever story."—*Atlas.*

"This is a well-drawn picture of life, and obviously from real personages and circumstances. Indeed, we recognise both, as must be the case with any one familiar with London for the last forty years. Bankers, men of fashion, fox and fortune-hunters, &c. &c., figure in the page, and the various turns in their fortunes and misfortunes furnish ample matter for the novelist, of which he has availed himself so as to excite considerable interest, and bring forth singular characters, as well as illustrate the conduct of worldlings in a striking manner."—*Literary Gazette.*

II.

CAPTAIN GLASSCOCK'S LAND SHARKS AND SEA GULLS.

Three Volumes.

With Illustrations by GEORGE CRUIKSHANK.

"A work of first-rate merit, full of humour, and replete with incidents which show a general understanding of mankind."—*John Bull.*

"We heartily recommend this novel to our readers. It abounds in characteristic sketches, done, doubtless, from originals, with a dry and biting touch of satire."—*Morning Chronicle.*

III.

MRS. TROLLOPE'S ROMANCE OF VIENNA.

Three Volumes. Second Edition.

"Without doubt the best of Mrs. Trollope's novels."—*Spectator.*
"A cleverly written novel, full of lively and romantic scenes."—*Athenæum.*

IV.

MR. COOPER'S HOMEWARD BOUND.

Three Volumes. New Edition.

"Mr. Cooper has again pushed off into blue water, and is once again the hearty, vigorous man, 'roughing it' on the wild element which has been his nursing mother. 'Homeward Bound' is one of his capital sea-stories. The liveliness of its painting, and the interest it excites, place its author at the head of the fleet of fiction weavers."—*Athenæum.*

RICHARD BENTLEY, NEW BURLINGTON STREET.

THE CHEAPEST
LIBRARY OF ENTERTAINMENT
EVER PUBLISHED.

Now in course of publication, in neatly bound pocket volumes, price Six Shillings each, printed and embellished with Engravings, uniformly with the 'Waverley Novels,' to which they are suitable companions,

THE STANDARD NOVELS
AND ROMANCES.

THIS COLLECTION NOW COMPRISES THE BEST WORKS

OF THE FOLLOWING

MOST DISTINGUISHED MODERN NOVELISTS:

COOPER, CAPTAIN MARRYAT, HOPE, MISS EDGEWORTH, BECKFORD, G. P. R. JAMES, SIR E. L. BULWER, BART., MISS AUSTEN, AINSWORTH, MRS. BRUNTON, GODWIN, THEODORE HOOK, MISSES LEE, MORIER, MADAME DE STAEL, MANZONI, BANIM, VICTOR HUGO, MRS. INCHBALD, MRS. SHELLEY, GALT, MRS. GORE, HORACE WALPOLE, SCHILLER, MISSES PORTER, GRATTAN, GLEIG, WASHINGTON IRVING, HORACE SMITH, M. G. LEWIS, CHATEAUBRIAND, MAXWELL, PEACOCK, &c.

Vol.
1. THE PILOT, by Cooper.
2. CALEB WILLIAMS, by Godwin.
3. THE SPY, by Cooper.
4. THADDEUS OF WARSAW, by Miss Jane Porter.
5. ST. LEON, by Godwin.
6. LAST OF THE MOHICANS, by Cooper.
7 and 8. THE SCOTTISH CHIEFS, by Miss Jane Porter.
9. FRANKENSTEIN, by Mrs. Shelley; and GHOST SEER, Vol. I. by Schiller.
10. EDGAR HUNTLY, by Brockden Brown; and Conclusion of GHOST SEER.
11. HUNGARIAN BROTHERS, by Miss A. M. Porter.
12 and 13. CANTERBURY TALES, by the Misses Lee.
14. THE PIONEERS, by Cooper.
15. SELF CONTROL, by Mrs. Brunton.
16. DISCIPLINE, by Mrs. Brunton.

Vol.
17. THE PRAIRIE, by Cooper.
18 and 19. THE PASTOR'S FIRE-SIDE, by Miss Jane Porter.
20. LIONEL LINCOLN, by Cooper.
21. LAWRIE TODD, by Galt.
22. FLEETWOOD, by Godwin.
23. SENSE AND SENSIBILITY, by Miss Austen.
24. CORINNE, by Madame de Stael.
25. EMMA, by Miss Austen.
26. SIMPLE STORY, and NATURE AND ART, by Mrs. Inchbald.
27. MANSFIELD PARK, by Miss Austen.
28. NORTHANGER ABBEY, and PERSUASION, by Miss Austen.
29. THE SMUGGLER, by Banim.
30. PRIDE AND PREJUDICE, by Miss Austen.
31. STORIES OF WATERLOO, by Maxwell.
32. THE HUNCHBACK OF NOTRE DAME, by Victor Hugo.

STANDARD NOVELS.

Vol.
33. THE BORDERERS, by *Cooper.*
34. EUGENE ARAM, by *Bulwer.*
35. MAXWELL, by *Theodore Hook.*
36. WATER WITCH, by *Cooper.*
37. MOTHERS & DAUGHTERS, by *Mrs. Gore.*
38. THE BRAVO, by *Cooper.*
39. THE HEIRESS OF BRUGES, by *Grattan.*
40. RED ROVER, by *Cooper.*
41. VATHEK, by *Beckford;* CASTLE OF OTRANTO, by *H. Walpole;* and BRAVO OF VENICE, by *M. G. Lewis.*
42. THE COUNTRY CURATE, by *Gleig.*
43. THE BETROTHED, by *Manzoni.*
44. HAJJI BABA, by *Morier.*
45. HAJJI BABA IN ENGLAND, by *Morier.*
46. THE PARSON'S DAUGHTER, by *Theodore Hook.*
47. PAUL CLIFFORD, by *Bulwer.*
48. THE YOUNGER SON, by *Capt. Trelawny.*
49. THE ALHAMBRA, by *Washington Irving;* THE LAST OF THE ABENCERRAGES, by *Chateaubriand;* and THE INVOLUNTARY PROPHET, by *Horace Smith.*

Vol.
50. THE HEADSMAN, by *Cooper.* and 52. ANASTASIUS, by *Hope.*
53. DARNLEY, by *James.*
54. ZOHRAB, by *Morier.*
55. HEIDENMAUER, by *Cooper.*
56. DE L'ORME, by *James.*
57. HEADLONG HALL, NIGHTMARE ABBEY, MAID MARIAN, and CROTCHET CASTLE, by *Peacock.*
58. TREVELYAN, *by the Author of "A Marriage in High Life."*
59. PHILIP AUGUSTUS, by *James.*
60. ROOKWOOD, by *Ainsworth.*
61. HENRY MASTERTON, by *James.*
62. PETER SIMPLE, by *Marryat.*
63. JACOB FAITHFUL, by *Marryat.*
64. JAPHET IN SEARCH OF A FATHER, by *Marryat.*
65. KING'S OWN, by *Marryat.*
66. MR. MIDSHIPMAN EASY, by *Marryat.*
67. NEWTON FORSTER, by *Marryat.*
68. THE PACHA OF MANY TALES, by *Marryat.*
69. RATTLIN THE REEFER.
70. ADVENTURES OF CAPTAIN BLAKE, by *Maxwell.*
71. HELEN, by *Miss Edgeworth.*

To be followed by

SIR E. BULWER'S "LAST DAYS OF POMPEII;"

Captain Chamier's "Life of a Sailor," and "Ben Brace;" Miss Mitford's "Belford Regis;" Mrs. Trollope's "Jonathan Jefferson Whitlaw," and other popular works of the most distinguished modern writers of fiction.

_{*} Any volume may be had separately, containing a complete work, (*in all but four instances,*) price Six Shillings.

The Works which form "THE STANDARD NOVELS," being the Copyright of MR. BENTLEY, can only be procured in that Series, *which is wholly unconnected with any other Collection of Novels whatever.*

"We know of no recent work that deserves so hearty an encouragement from the great body of English readers. From the first issue to the present moment we have never ceased to recommend the 'Standard Novels,'—it is an unrivalled series of modern works of fiction."—*Athenæum.*

RICHARD BENTLEY, NEW BURLINGTON STREET, LONDON.

*** TO BE HAD, ALSO, OF ALL BOOKSELLERS IN THE UNITED KINGDOM.

Dickens Charles

Oliver Twist

Tome 1

Richard Bentley

1839

Y2 27423

www.ingramcontent.com/pod-product-compliance
Lightning Source LLC
Chambersburg PA
CBHW060453170426
43199CB00011B/1188